Pastor Served Al Dente

Pastor Served Al Dente

A Layman's Search for the Perfect Pastor

EDGAR STUBBERSFIELD

Foreword by Fred Kornis

RESOURCE *Publications* · Eugene, Oregon

PASTOR SERVED AL DENTE
A Layman's Search for the Perfect Pastor

Resource Publications
An Imprint of Wipf and Stock Publishers
199 W. 8th Ave., Suite 3
Eugene, OR 97401

www.wipfandstock.com

PAPERBACK ISBN: 978-1-6667-3862-9
HARDCOVER ISBN: 978-1-6667-9955-2
EBOOK ISBN: 978-1-6667-9956-9

05/31/23

This book honors the memory of two men who showed me what Jesus is like, Cecil Seymore of Gatton Congregational Church and Bryn Barrett, of Toowoomba Assembly of God Church.

They both now stand in God's presence and see clearly what they reflected to me when I was young. May you be blessed to know such men.

Contents

Foreword by Fred Kornis   ix

Introduction   xi

A Vocation not a Profession   1

Integrity and Gifting   8

The Importance of Developing a Strong Character   21

Someone Who Forgives   27

Preaching to the Heart not the Head   31

A Person of Undivided Attention   44

A Person with Compassion for the Weak   53

The Servant of All   58

Someone Who Listens   66

What Really Goes Wrong   71

Questions to Ask a Potential Pastor   77

Bibliography   81

Foreword

IT HAS BEEN MY distinct honor and privilege to know Edgar Stubbersfield in action on three continents of the world. He is a sensitive scholar and a beloved Christian brother. Few, in our superficial and distracted generation, have any clue of the eternal and infinite place "Pastors" play in God's glorious plans.

As my heart burned, reading this book, a fresh awareness and appreciation for the unique role of local pastors hit me. How quickly our modern world has lost all perspective and community benefits of pastors. The concept of a CALLING, in any vocation, has almost disappeared. In the realms of religious ministry, there has been, since ancient times, the idea of a hireling . . . someone who only works for money. Today we would say a person only shows up and goes to work to get a paycheck. What a pitiful motivation! God help the employers who have employees like that. When we consider all the mainstream denominations across the world, and all the clergy and ministers involved, if they also are only in it for the money, we would have a perverted and corrupted church.

This compelling and engaging book, dealing with a true sincere "calling" for those who handle and teach the sacred scriptures, is long overdue! You will see and sense throughout this work that SCRIPTURE is the ultimate measure for reality. Lacing and weaving throughout this book are names like John Wesley, Martin Luther, Charles Finney, Jonathan Edwards, Billy Graham, JC Ryle, and others who reveal the wonder and practical effects of God's calling for pastors. The "down under" Australian humor is sprinkled throughout this book with wisdom and wit.

As religious institutions, organizations, systems, and churches continue to drift dangerously into subtle secular and woke cultures. This book must be required reading for all pastors and church leaders.

Dr. Frederick Kornis
Heartland International Ministries
Kansas City, USA

Introduction

Pastor Served al Dente . . . what kind of a title is that? *The Seven Pillars of Wisdom,* one of the great books in the English language, is T. E. Lawrence's (Lawrence of Arabia) account of the Arab uprising during World War One. Someone asked him what the title meant. He replied that he had no idea. It was just a great title. Well, at least my title was good enough to have you read this far. And it is probably a whole lot better than *Roast Pastor for Sunday Lunch* though, heaven knows, how many times that dish has been served. As for the subtitle, *A Layman's Search for the Perfect Pastor,* I learnt a long time ago that the quest for such a being will be as fruitless as the search for the elusive bunyip.[1] But a good pastor? That is an entirely different matter; they do exist but may well be a threatened species. This book is intended to set a very high yet, with God's help, still achievable bar for anyone considering Christian ministry. However, while it is a gentle reminder to the church about what a pastor should be, this book is also a gentle reminder to the pastor of what a member should be like!

When I was a much younger man I sat and shared heart to heart with one of my state's leading evangelists. What he told me that night shocked me. He said, "It is the easiest thing in the world to start a new church; the hardest thing is finding it a good pastor." I am now certain that the evangelist overstated the simplicity of starting a church but, in my advancing age, I fear that he understated the difficulty in getting it a good pastor. Yet, difficult as it may be, it is

---

1. A creature from aboriginal mythology that lives in creeks and billabongs (i.e., an oxbow lake).

not impossible. This evangelist had an uncle named Cecil Seymore, a name all but long forgotten and Cecil is now dust. Yet, he lives on. After visiting the old Congregational manse in my home town, his onetime home, an auntie of mine spoke of him saying that after thirty years she could still sense his godly presence in the building. Be that as it may, he was my father in the Christian faith and showed me what Christ is like. I tried to model my life on his example so, in a sense, he does live on in this world as well as the other.

I remember vividly how he came to our Congregational church. We were without a minister and the moderator brought a bright young man straight out of college for our consideration. He followed the "God is Dead" theology, we were told. But our church could not afford to pay the services of a professional man, so he was declined. No one questioned his theology! Next, we were offered Cecil, an old Presbyterian minister. He was too old to be allowed to continue to minister in that denomination, but the Congo's would be glad to have him if he was cheap. And he was. He worked for the pension with a top up from the church to run the car. Despite that, he worked with a zeal that would leave a younger man dead in his tracks. He loved and guided me in my newfound faith. I have thanked the Good Lord many times that I was nurtured by such a man and not a young liberal with a doubtful experience of a living and loving savior.

This book discusses a range of topics at the core of Christian ministry but there could be many, many, more. The style and length of the chapters vary considerably. As for the topics themselves, each could easily be the subject of a tome rather than a few pages but, hopefully, I have grasped the nub of the subject. While there is a temptation to mention living tele-evangelists with big homes, private jets, designer suits, and expensive cars, when I started this book a wise friend told me, "Don't get sued." A principle of British law which Australia follows is that you cannot defame the dead! Accordingly, a common theme through the chapters is to use historical examples to illustrate the point I am trying to make. You have my permission to mentally substitute names known to you.

While I have been blessed to encounter some amazing pastors, I have also suffered under some that were truly appalling! I had to stop myself from allowing this small book degenerating into a winge[2] about the damage they and so many others have done. Instead, I concentrate on a celebration of what was good. I hope that the following chapters give you something to think about and encourage you to live a remarkable life. As mentioned earlier, those who sit in the pews don't get a free ride as the aspects of ministry that I explore almost universally apply to the congregation also.

2. An Australianism for a whining complaint.

A Vocation not a Profession

I AM A MEMBER of a small Baptist church in the middle of a potato field near my hometown of Gatton in country Queensland.[1] It is situated about one and a half hour's drive from our state capital, Brisbane. Alternatively, it is two hours from Surfers Paradise in the heart of the Gold Coast, our main tourist strip. My church is financially viable. The members have loved their pastors. We have a modern chapel, and we have the best Baptist manse in Queensland. A few years ago, we were looking to call a new pastor. The Baptist Union informed us that this might not be an easy thing as most pastors would not accept a call to a country church. It seems that the Good Lord's call seemed to stop about half an hour's drive from the coast. Strange that!

Here is another scenario from class conscious nineteenth century Britain. There, many farmers had sufficient land to provide a very comfortable living, but they worked their land which excluded them from the "landed gentry." These people who worked for a living were considered "in trade." As for the gentry, the eldest son inherited the land and title but what do you do with the younger sons? There were a few professions that were not demeaning for their social status. These were the officer corps of the British army for the second son, law for the third son and, way down the list was the clergy of the established church for the fourth (or sometimes the least intelligent) son.

The third setting could not be more different from the first two examples. In 1970, I was introduced to the very undeveloped

---

1. Check out *Sermons from a Potato Field* also published by Wipf and Stock.

developing world and its associated poverty. However, I was fortunate enough to do this as an onlooker from the comfort of luxury accommodation, servants, security guards and new vehicles. In about 1995, I went to speak at a conference in General Santos City, the bombing capital of Southern Mindanao in the Philippines. The delegates were mainly poor tribal pastors. For the first time, I lived among poverty and rubbed shoulders with the desperately poor. One of the leaders told me about the faithfulness of their pastors. I call them pastors, though they had virtually no training, but they were the only ones who would go into the hills! Those coming from the hills to study never wanted to return to that hard life! Yet, these untrained men so loved Christ and his church that they would go with their family to the remotest tribes. There may be no roads, and their children would be denied a decent education and health care. One of that denomination's leaders told me that all they asked for was vitamins! I had the honor of purchasing a pressure lamp for one of these pastors. He was a former guerrilla and had the opportunity of having Bible studies with the guerillas at night. That pressure lamp represented nine months of offerings from the church!

The same job but totally different expectations and motivations and commitments was driving their life choices. What drives yours or that of the pastor who serves you?

My father with his Hotchkiss machine gun in 1938

Before exploring the concept of calling, let me tell you a family story. My father was a light horseman. For foreign readers, the Australian light horse resplendent in their slouch hat with emu feather, were mounted infantry, and their exploits entered the psyche of our nation. Their battles include the horrors of Gallipoli in Turkey, the capture of Beersheba with one of the last cavalry charges in history followed by 800 of these men going on to take Jerusalem. They then raced and beat Lawrence of Arabia to capture Damascus. These bushmen from the youngest country were foundational in the establishment of Israel. The Gatton troop of "weekend warriors" were the best in the country as, in 1938, they won the Prince of Wales cup, the prize for which the light horse troops Australia wide competed. It was the largest silver cup in the world, so big you could easily bathe a baby in it.[2] My father was the regimental marksman and Australian champion machine gunner. The following year, war came, and the whole troop went off to enlist. My father did not pass the health test as he had a heart murmur, (and it did kill him fifty years later) so he was offered the role as an officer's batman or as a guard in Australia. Very unceremoniously, he told them what they could do with that. However, my father was a building contractor and a very good one at that. He enlisted in the Civil Construction Corps and was the foreman in charge of the construction of Amberley in Queensland, a major US Army Air Force base and then was moved on to Gatton Agricultural College to build the primary military hospital supporting General Macarthur's Southwest Pacific campaign.

This was a difficult time for him as he was young, looked fit and was fit and had skills the infantry desperately needed in North Africa and then New Guinea. Instead of firing bullets, I saw a letter from the War Department addressed to my father. It was accompanied by a set of plans for a new toilet block for the hospital. The letter instructed him to build it as a matter of urgency, and when he had time send a quote! On the fourth time he went to enlist, the officer took him aside and spoke sternly to him saying, "Don't you understand that the quickest way we will lose this war is if people like you go off to fight it! You are needed in Australia, be content to

2. It contained 15 kg of silver and measured a meter across.

3

do your bit here." Just as my dear old dad had to understand where his country needed him, so you must know where God actually wants you, not where you think he should place you, and be content there. This may well be the obscurity of a country parish serving those he loved so dearly that he died for them.

We can think of the ministry as the pinnacle of Christian service and that if we want to serve our Lord wholeheartedly, it can only be through full time work. While we might deny that is the case, the expectation can lie very deep. Even Charles Spurgeon fell into this trap. After telling his students that the desire for ministry should totally absorb them, he put it this way:

> If any student in this room could be content to be a newspaper editor, or a grocer, or a farmer, or a doctor, or a lawyer, or a senator, or a king, in the name of heaven and earth let him go his way; he is not the man in whom dwells the Spirit of God in its fullness, for a man so filled with God would utterly weary of any pursuit but that for which his inmost soul pants.[3]

I am sorry Charles, but in this matter at least you are wrong! The one in whom the Spirit dwells in its fullness is more likely to be the one who serves well in the vocation God has called him/her to. And this may or may not be full time ministry at home or on the mission field. As for myself, I had a dramatic conversion, was theologically trained, could occasionally preach very well and occasionally write well. I even had a theological library the likes of which most ministers would be envious but pretend not to be. I had also been conscious of what I thought was a "call" and had the desire to minister. Shouldn't I be in the ministry? Yet, it was patently obvious to me that I did not have the necessary gifts to be a good minister. Unfortunately, I had this terrible feeling of guilt about being a sawmiller and not a pastor and having settled for the less spiritual and less blessed path. One day, my old mentor took me to hear a professor from Germany, Hans Schwarz, who the Lutheran church in Australia brought out to celebrate 500 years since the birth of Luther. I was transfixed when he spoke about

3. Spurgeon, *Lectures to My Students,* 42.

Luther's concept of vocation and was finally able to be settled and know my calling.

The professor reminded us that the apostle Paul spoke of God's call extending to all believers (Rom 11:29; 1 Cor 1:26, Latin *vocatio* and *vocationem* respectively) but by the late Middle Ages the term vocation was reserved for monks. Luther upended this belief by "relating it to the worldly activities in which each individual is involved."[4] He did not elevate secular work but rather removed the idea that being a monk (or dare I say a pastor) put that person in a privileged position with a higher level of sanctification. Luther removed the distinction between secular and religious work whereby a person must be called out of the world to serve God.

He went on by reminding us that for the justified person, Christianity is not just intellectual assent but a response to God's service to us. All activities of any Christian should be directly related to God to whom ultimate loyalty was rendered.[5] The only decision, no matter how lowly the work might be, is whether "this kind of life is pleasing to God because it was instituted by him."[6] If it was instituted by God, then to look down on any vocation is to dishonor the creator. Luther very correctly emphasized vocation as service to one's neighbor which went far beyond paid work but included all the activities of life, work, family and private.[7] Luther reminded believers that life is multi-dimensional where we live in the home, the state and the church and our interpersonal relations vary in each of the stations, but none of them is "secular." While we may be employed, it should not just be a job. Our divine calling to glorify God and serve our neighbor is meant to be demonstrated in all our actions even our work.[8] This runs counter to the individualistic, self-centered and self-glorification that is seen in the lives of many today, including Christians and even ministers. To this day, the saintliest person I know was not a pastor but a council truck

4. Schwartz, "Martin Luther's Understanding," 4.
5. Schwartz, "Martin Luther's Understanding," 4–5.
6. Schwartz, "Martin Luther's Understanding," 5.
7. Schwartz, "Martin Luther's Understanding," 6.
8. Schwartz, "Martin Luther's Understanding," 5–6.

driver who completely embodied service to others. Having work as a vocation is certainly more difficult to achieve when someone is employed in a soul destroying, repetitive, high paced assembly line but that does not change what it is supposed to be and even can be.

Alongside the equality of the different stations of life, Luther had the understanding that all believers are called to the ecclesiastical office, whether it be a father instructing his son or a pastor instructing a church. However, there was also the additional understanding that God singles out individuals for specific tasks of service to others. There are two preconditions, the need in the community and the necessary education and qualifications to fulfil the role.

I went away transformed. I was content that my business was not a second-rate option that would deny me a closer relationship to my Heavenly Father. I was already good at sawmilling and got better as I understood that my primary role was to bless my customers through serving them. Later I specialized in weather exposed timber structures and went on to master the intricacies of designing them in a way that few in my country could match. Engineers would say, "You are the only person I can trust." I had found my vocation. In my retirement, I believe the Lord impressed upon me the need to write down what I had learnt so the next generation need not learn it again. As for all my study, that day the professor gave a very good quotation from Luther, "It never hurt a cobbler to learn Latin." Likewise, my study did not hurt me, nor will it hurt you.

If you are weighing whether you are being singled out by God for Christian ministry, you need to fully understand that it is not a calling to a better, more spiritual life but simply to a different vocation. Heaven forbid that you ever think that because God loves the shepherd, he will give them sheep. There must be the opposite understanding, that because God loves the sheep, he gives them a shepherd. Then there can be a start to a healthy understanding of ministry as a calling and something you should give your life to. The prospective pastor should be looking externally, not internally. Personally, I would question the validity of a call to the ministry if someone introduced into that mix a desire for power, or a desire for a higher spiritual life. The church has been troubled enough by such people.

While I have stressed the role of the minister as a vocation which requires of him/her that he/she elevates and honors the vocations of his/her members, I am not suggesting that the members dishonor the pastor. The office of minister should be one that holds respect in and of itself, yet that trust has been sorely abused. We now live in an individualistic and democratic society where a pastor does not automatically have respect given. Trust and respect now more than ever need to be earned and this is best done on a person-to-person basis. A pastor who has achieved this is one who is worthy of double honor, for first taking on that role and the second for fulfilling the role well (1 Tim 5:7). When they have a heart like God's heart (Jer 3:1), and they speak the gospel faithfully with matching actions, their members can have confidence in them. Submitting to them should not be a burden. They have an awesome responsibility as they must give an account to their maker for the flock they have been called to watch over. Yet this role is not meant to be a burden but a joy (Heb 13:17). The following chapters give insights into what this poor old sawmiller considers a vocation of full-time service to God's kingdom should look like. It is not an easy life, but if you will walk humbly with your God, it will be a blessed one but demand everything of you.

Integrity and Gifting

THE ROYAL COMMISSION INTO *Institutional Responses to Child Abuse* in Australia brought to light the most depraved acts against the most vulnerable by the most trusted. A significant number[1] of "ministers of the Gospel" were proven to have been no more than traitors to the faith. Churches that put their reputation ahead of their pastoral duty have been shamed to the extent that it is hard to see how they will ever recover. I have a friend who was the lead architect at a major Queensland firm and, at the time of writing, his company was designing a church school. One of the requirements was that there will be a clear glass or Perspex wall separating the priest from any student. How has the church fallen so low? But this is not the first time that the church has had to confront the effects of ministers working without integrity. It goes to the earliest days when Simon Magus thought the gifts of God could be purchased with money (Acts 8:9–24) and when Paul had to send Timothy to Ephesus to confront "leaders" who were leading people astray for their own personal gain (1 Tim 6:5).

There is nothing new under the sun as this has been seen repeatedly through church history. Consider the situation in England after their Reformation. Laws were passed that deprived sincere Christians of the pastors they trusted and forced them to attend the parish church. There the priest had flip flopped with every change that Henry, Edward, Mary, and Elizabeth had imposed, yet

---

1. The Commission received 67,000 calls, letters, and emails, held 8,000 private sessions, and made 2,500 referrals to the police. Most were from church institutions. Royal Commission, "Home page," par 1.

they were known to be papists at heart. As well, their morals and their intellectual grasp of the scriptures could be seriously wanting.[2] Such men were held in contempt and amid this scandalous situation many were asking, "How valid is a sacrament performed by such a person?" Were their children's baptism even recognized by God? The Anglican Church answered this question with Article Twenty-six of their Thirty-nine Articles where it acknowledges that corruption could reach to the very top offices of the church but encouraged the faithful that the sacraments were gifts from God, not a man. Their answer is theoretically and theologically true but, "it could not control those instincts and sympathies which really govern the majority of mankind in such matters."[3]

Neither should it satisfy any reasonable person. The old theologian I just quoted hit the nail squarely on the head when he went on to say, "All who are earnest about religion know that the life of the pastor setting forth the life of Christ which he preaches is the most eloquent and persuasive illustration of the truth."[4] He reminded the students that studied his book of theology that nothing can hold a church together other than the "personal character and influence of an enlightened clergy."[5] Ultimately, the church is Christ's church and it is his responsibility to hold it together and this is often done through the spirituality and commitment of the lay leaders and members. But the church should prosper, not merely survive.

Today, the public expectation (and even perhaps increasingly now the Christian expectation) is that the leader may well not have the fundamental and essential attribute of integrity. On top of the reticence to trust such people, many ministers may now come from cultures and lifestyles that bear little resemblance to the ones they now minister in. This means they can have trouble fully connecting with their congregation and their congregation with them. To some

---

2. When Bishop Hooper made a survey of 311 of his clergy in the diocese of Gloucester in 1563 he discovered that 186 could not recite the ten commandments, thirty-four did not know who said the Lord's Prayer and ten could not recite it! Manning, "Spread of the Popular Reformation," 41.

3. Boultbee, *Theology*, 221.

4. Boultbee, *Theology*, 221.

5. Boultbee, *Theology*, 221.

extent, no doubt unintentionally, some denominations are seeing certain of their priests virtually sidelined as "functionaries." They are needed for the administration of the sacraments, but a spiritual and trained lay workers are, in effect, responsible for the healthy running of the church.

But it shouldn't be either/or where one compensates for the other. I remember, growing up as a Congregationalist in my small town, how we could look askance at Roman Catholics, but no one would dare voice a word of criticism of their parish priest, Father Cahill. Everyone knew he was a man of the people, a lover of sport, yet at the same time a man of God who exuded integrity.

There is no *Dummy's Guide to Integrity* so how does anyone possess this personal character, this integrity? This is not something that is meant to be the possession of the pastor only but it is his role is to display it so others may follow. In Father Cahill's case I expect it had a lot to do with working with a man of integrity when he was fresh out of seminary, Father Walsh. (Our town only had two priests over a ninety-year period). What made his mentor faithful? I expect again that it had a lot to do with remaining faithful when God himself appeared unfaithful and unknowable! My grandfather built his new church in 1889. On the last day of construction, the one the congregation had so looked forward to and sacrificed for, he sent a young builder up on the roof to install the cross. Tragically, he lost his grip and fell to his death. The questions that tragedy raised were nothing in comparison to what would happen a few short years later.

Father Walsh would be in the midst the biggest murder en-quiry in Queensland's history[6] when in 1898 three siblings, from a very small and close community, were brutally murdered and their murderer never found. The mother of the two girls and their brother was apparently one of his most devout communicants. Then there was the pastoral role dealing with the dreadful losses of World War One which hit our community very hard. Mediocrity breeds mediocrity, and Father Walsh as a mentor could never be accused of that. This man was forged in fire as we could only pray

---

6. Wikipedia has a very accurate article on this entitled, "Gatton Murders."

we never will be. There is an aspect to the integrity of a pastor that is not a matter of weeks and months or even of years but should be the work of generations.

Equally important is the personal aspect of integrity. Having a mentor with integrity means nothing if a person's spirit is inflexible and refuses to be molded. When I was a young student pastor, I met Father Cahill and he spoke to me, not as a died in the wool Catholic to one of the "separated brethren," but with a pastor's heart. He questioned me on my prayer life and told me that this is where the pastor's work was done. This very public figure had a private life that only his Lord knew. I would have been wise to have followed his advice and prayed more. But in the final washup, apart from turning bread and wine into the physical body and blood of Christ, I am sure he would not have called himself "gifted."

Something that is not the work of the influence of preceding generations and of a lifetime of personal discipline is the subject of gifting for ministry and the means of acquiring integrity is not an easy subject to pin down. Neither is gifting which can seem to come unrelated to that continuing foundation. It is very difficult to define gifting as where does natural ability end and divine assistance starts. The old adage, "It is better felt than telt," certainly applies here. The remainder of this chapter explores the spectacular gifts, for lack of a better word and then the seemingly ordinary.

Gifting is a subject usually associated with the Pentecostal branch of the church so we will consider this story from early Australian Pentecostal history. It is longer than the other illustration in this book, but the story is complex and profound in its implications. Please bear with me as I tell it In 1909 Janet Lancaster's "Good News Hall," with links to the holiness movement, became the first Pentecostal assembly in Australia. Her group had no connection with the Assemblies of God, founded in 1914 in the USA[7] and the later Australian Pentecostal Church. Unfortunately, Good News Hall proclaimed serious doctrinal errors concerning Christology and divine judgment. Some of its practices also embodied the worst

---

7. Mc Klung, *Azusa Street*, 19.

of Pentecostalism. These doctrines would divorce this group from what would become the mainstream Pentecostal churches.

In 1926, a South African evangelist from the *Apostolic Faith Mission*,[8] Frederick Van Eyk, along with his wife and family, came to Australia. Later in the year, when other evangelists were dissociating themselves from Mrs. Lancaster, he joined with Good News Hall.[9] The Hall, and its associated churches, adopted the name *Apostolic Faith Mission*.[10] At their first conference in 1927, Van Eyk was appointed "First Evangelist." Pentecostalism was starting to be organized and began to grow rapidly under Van Eyk's tireless endeavors. He ministered in every state but especially in Queensland. Wherever Van Eyk preached, conversions and dramatic healings were reported, even in the newspapers, and churches were established. The reported healings went far beyond what would be possible through suggestion and psychosomatic illnesses and included deafness and blindness.[11]

Mrs. Lancaster who had ministered with Smith Wigglesworth and seen Amie McPherson and leading Australian evangelists said, "Never have we seen such wonderful anointings of the Spirit as have been vouchsafed to Brother Van Eyk."[12] One "veteran Pentecostal elder" said of his preaching that as he "unfolds the mystery of God's Holy Word, you are lost in wonder and adoration, are just carried away on a higher plane into the presence of God."[13] Van Eyk believed that scripture was to be believed and experienced[14] and encouraged

---

8 This group had roots in Dowieism and in 1984 was one of the largest Pentecostal groups in South Africa, Chant, *Heart of Fire*, 88. John Alexander Dowie (1847–1907) was an Australian Congregational Minister who is largely credited with pioneering faith healing.

9. Lancaster, "Good News," September 1926, 11.

10. Lancaster, "Good News," November 1926, 10.

11. Van Eyk, "The South African Evangelists' Report," 20–21. See also *Good News* September 1926, 12 and September 1927, 12 for staggering lists of dramatic healings. Chant elaborates on these, many of which were reported in newspapers or letters written by the person healed. The fact of the healing was not disputed, just the method. Chant, *Spirit*, 286.

12. Lancaster, "Fellowship with God," 15.

13. Lancaster, "First Impressions," 18.

14. Chant, *Spirit*, 292.

this through preaching a foursquare gospel of conversion, divine healing, the second coming, and the baptism in the Holy Spirit.[15] His meetings appear free of unseemly behavior reported from some historical revivalist meetings.[16]

In 1928, at the height of his success, Van Eyk held a month-long mission in Toowoomba[17] establishing a church. Unfortunately, Van Eyk's marriage was in trouble,[18] and his wife, (who had a mental health break down) and their children returned to South Africa. The evangelist made Toowoomba his base. Barry Chant, a Pentecostal historian, asks if there were already signs of recklessness and arrogance[19] as Mrs. Lancaster wrote the extraordinary words, "The change [to a] widely sought after evangelist, approved by God by the mighty signs and wonder . . . , is one which places him in a precarious position; for the plaudits of the people are likely to become a dangerous asset; many of God's favored and gifted messengers have fallen through pride. So, beloved, do not fail to surround him with such a wall of prayer that Satan and all his hosts shall find it impossible to break through."[20]

In 1928 he fell ill there and was nursed back to health by the pastor's daughter. Chant[21] described what happened, "It became increasingly obvious that this was more than a platonic relationship. Christians who at first sought to believe only the best soon found it impossible to believe anything but the worst. Slowly, their doubts became fears and fears became anger." The church split with Van Eyk's supporters forming the Elim Foursquare church and the others taking the name Assembly of God (AOG) (its first use in Australia but now known as Australian Christian Churches). Van Eyk continued to hold meetings even after his tent was burnt down

15. Chant, *Spirit*, 288.

16. Chant, *Spirit*, 312.

17. Queensland's largest regional center, about 130 km west of Brisbane, sited on the edge of the Darling Downs.

18. His wife appeared to have continued mental health problems and the marriage is generally regarded to have been a sham. Chant, *Heart of Fire*, 115.

19. Chant, *Spirit*, 298.

20. Lancaster, "Good News," 18:5, 10.

21. Chant, *Heart of Fire*, 113.

and large open-air meetings blocked the streets. As discontent grew, he was "literally put out of the town."[22] After Van Eyk rejected all advice to alter his ways and be reunited with his wife, his name was struck off the roll of the Mission early in 1929.

The impact of Van Eyk's fall was so severe that most Queensland churches affiliated with the Good News Hall dropped the name.[23] Later, in 1929, seventeen Queensland leaders met in Brisbane to formally discuss a new name and adopted "The Assemblies of God (Queensland), apparently unaware of its use in the USA.[24] This was a complete break with Good News Hall for they renounced the "principles of Christadelphianism"[25] held by some of its leaders. The AOG's (Qld) statement of faith was completely orthodox. The door had now been opened that would eventually lead to the present acceptance of the AOG by most Australian Christians, but this would still take many years.

Van Eyk continued preaching in the southern states. In mid-1929, he held a series of evangelistic meetings in the coalfields at Cessnock. This was during the depression years with first a miners' strike and then a lockout and, in these desperate times the families were living on rabbits. The Communist leaders were promoting direct action, explosives were stockpiled, and authorities contemplated calling out the militia. The meetings were no ordinary evangelistic outreach. The local paper reported that his meetings were viewed by Welsh residents who had seen that revival as its equal. Hundreds had been converted and many had been healed including a number regaining their vision and one woman who had "not walked for years was able to walk at the bidding of the evangelist."[26] These meetings were successful to the point that the Communists lost so many members that they never regained their influence. The explosives stockpile was revealed. The son of the commanding officer of the infantry battalion stationed there at the time said, "This

22. Chant, *Heart of Fire*, 114.

23. Chant, *Spirit*, 299.

24 The AOG (Qld.) joined with the Pentecostal Church of Australia in 1935 to become the Assembly of God (AOG).

25. Nichol, *The Pentecostals*, 173.

26. "Evangelistic and Healing Campaign," 5.

revival may have saved Australia from a bloody revolution."[27] Van Eyk founded an assembly in the town called the *Church of the Four Square Gospel.*

Van Eyk returned to South Africa in 1933 where he protested his innocence with his peers who decided he had suffered unjustly at the hands of the Australians and consequently clearing him of any wrongdoing. He returned to Australia with his family in 1934 and with other South African pastors, started to establish a denomination initially called the Elim Foursquare Church.[28] Van Eyk's use of the UK and New Zealand Pentecostal Group's name was not authorized. Discussions were held about affiliating. Two Elim evangelists almost travelled to Australia in the 1930's to minister. Ultimately, being made aware of Van Eyk's history the denomination refused to affiliate with him.[29] His first marriage failed, after which he had a breakdown. Van Eyk then married his young lady from Toowoomba.

In 1939, Van Eyk and his brother went hunting in South Africa and both were bitten by a tzetse fly and contracted sleeping sickness. While his brother took medical treatment, Van Eyk did not, believing it was in conflict with his preaching of divine healing. While his brother survived, the pioneer of Australian Pentecostal evangelism died. The manner of his death proved categorically that Van Eyk was not a charlatan or intended to deceive as he died by what he preached. His death was viewed in the Pentecostal circles as either a great tragedy or divine judgment!

The impact of this failed minister was so great that it would close the eyes of many to an honest appraisal and, for a long time, the AOG would remain for most Christians, (and on the Darling Downs particularly), a cult to be avoided.[30] In the forties, Pentecos-

---

27. Piggin, *Firestorm*, 69–70.

28. In 2022 there were eighty-one Foursquare churches listed on its Australian website http://www.foursquareaust.com.au.

29. Cartwright, Desmond, *Pers. Com.,* 2007.

30 The history of the Ravensbourne Methodist Church written C.1961 still described the AOG work there as divisive and with "disturbing elements of false teaching."

tals in Queensland would still be referred to as Van Eykers.[31] It is reasonable to state that, for the Downs, Van Eyk's sin was the biggest factor hindering Pentecostal church growth for many years, as one old member graphically said, "Our name was mud."[32] An old AOG pastor, described the prevailing atmosphere, "It wasn't so much opposition, but persecution, the churches were united in their opposition of us."[33] Through his own endeavors Van Eyk established two denominations, indirectly started another and most likely prevented the entry of a fourth, the legitimate owner of the Elim name, from starting in the country. In the end he was rejected by sinner and saint alike and we can only question what might have been.

The actions of the elders of the Toowoomba AOG were profound. They were standing in judgment of a man who was unrepentant, but more than that, they were standing in judgment of God, and I do not say that lightly. Van Eyk's God given gifts were obvious, but just as obvious to them was the reality that there was no matching integrity which showed believers and unbelievers alike how to live a holy life. In the midst of the competing and acknowledged claims of wonders on one hand and the need for a sincere holy life on the other, the elders had to decide what foundation their church would be built upon. They chose the latter. Was it an easy choice to appear to stand in judgment of God's "choice"? I don't think so, but it molded that church for generations to follow. It would sit outside of the normal AOG church in its orthodoxy through avoiding extremes and the latest trends.[34]

I wish I could say that the lessons from church leadership that lacked integrity were ones that were well learnt and put behind us

---

31. Averill, *Go North*, 70. In an interview with John Simmons, a retired Pentecostal pastor from Toowoomba in May 1996 he recounted his parent's horror that he had become a Pentecostal as they believed this was a group that tolerated immorality. Their belief was encouraged as Van Eyk had "run off with the daughter of a close friend" This incident is in keeping with the belief in the Toowoomba AOG that their young lady was the last of many (Jones *Pers. Com.*, 1996) and runs contrary to official AOG history books that play down or ignores the Toowoomba incident. Hunt, *Assemblies of God*, 31

32. Jones, Audrey. *Pers. Com.*, August 1996.

33. Hallop, Theo. *Pers. Com.*, August 1996

34. I was a member of this church for many years.

just as we have the heresies of old. Unfortunately, it is far from it. You have to have been living under a rock not to have been aware of the moral and/or financial failures of high-profile tele-evangelists and denomination leaders. Yet, how much of this flies under the radar? On the local level, thousands of churches have had to face the same issue of a loved and trusted pastor failing. The devastation it leaves in its wake can sometimes never be repaired. The Dissenters could easily and correctly have seen themselves fighting *for* God when they rejected the ministry of inept and immoral parish priests, but others were required to consider if they were fighting *against* God by rejecting those whom he had gifted. In a society that is loath to commit to anything, let alone absolutes in virtue, it is not a welcome message that integrity can only come from recognizing absolutes and commitment to them. It must be evident in the pastor but equally it must reside in the members as with those old English Dissenters and lay leadership like the Toowoomba AOG as well.

In the absence of this *Dummies Guide*, what should a young man or woman[35] seeking a life of ministry do to develop integrity? For that matter, any believer. As much as possible I would urge them to avoid mediocrity in their mentors and role models. We all need mentors so who do you choose? Mine came to me by "accident." I did not seek them out, but it is as if they sought me out. You should take the initiative in seeking someone to guide your formative years and don't be afraid to ask. And don't be afraid to let that person be someone from outside of your theological tradition. You will be surprised at the wisdom and depth that exists outside of the walls of your denomination. The parts that you do not have control over are the circumstances of life that God will bring you to and through. Combine God's forging in fire with wise counsel of a mentor and the strength of the Spirit and you will gain the integrity needed to be a valued and trusted minister of the gospel. This is no different whether you are behind or in front of the pulpit.

As for gifts, it is unlikely that you will cause the blind to see and the lame to walk though you would be seriously remiss if you did not ask your big God for big things. Nevertheless, there should

35. Refer to my book, *Women in Ministry,* published by Wipf and Stock for a defense of female ministry.

be a seal of God's approval upon a ministry that others recognize. We can tend to see the gifts of the Holy Spirit in the very limited scope of the nine gifts of the Spirit in First Corinthians chapter 12 as espoused by the Pentecostals. I look at the same list very differently. There are, in fact, six lists of gifts of the Spirit in that book, and they are not all the same. I have listed them in Table 1, but I have put a number beside each gift as it is first mentioned and used that same number whenever the gift is repeated. I found seventeen gifts. Agreed, some of these gifts are difficult to distinguish from others and you might get only sixteen or fifteen, but whatever it is it will be a lot more than nine. Some of them we would not necessarily see as "gifts" but "fruit" of the Spirit. I believe we do disservice to the notion of gifts if we see Paul's list is exhaustive. Some of these look just so ordinary to the extent that they could easily be overlooked as a gift.

Paul encouraged the Corinthians to seek the gifts and every minister of the gospel should be actively seeking an extra dimension to his or her ministry that transcends their own ability. Perhaps you are not conscious of any God given gifts. There is a lesson from this much shorter but equally profound story. The two big names of the 1850's revival in Wales were Humphrey Jones and David Morgan. Morgan, at first, was a sceptic but on hearing Jones speak was convinced of shortcomings in his ministry. At last David Morgan said to Jones, "There can be no harm in our attempting to rouse the churches of the region; I am willing to do my best. We can do no mischief by holding prayer meetings, though there should be no more than *man* in it all." "You do that," responded the other, "and I will guarantee that *God* will be with you very soon."[36] One night soon after, Daniel Morgan went to bed as usual, just a country pastor in a small town and woke in the morning and felt like there was a lion loose in him and which was accompanied by an incredible memory for spiritual things. Just as suddenly it left him two years later.[37]

---

36. Morgan, *The '59 Revival*, 10.

37. Morgan, *The '59 Revival*, 11–12.

	12:8–10		12:28		12:29–30
1	Speak with wisdom	10	Apostles	10	Apostles
2	Speak with knowledge	6	Prophets	12	Prophets
3	Faith	11	Teachers	11	Teachers
4	Gifts of healing	5	Miracle workers	5	Miracle workers
5	Miraculous powers	4	Healing gifts	4	Gifts of healing
6	Prophecy	12	Helping others	8	Different tongues
7	Distinguishing spirits	13	Administration	9	Interpreting tongues
8	Different tongues	8	Different tongues		
9	Interpreting tongues				
	13:1–3		14:6		14:26
8	Different tongues	8	Different tongues	16	Hymn
6	prophecy	2	Revelation	11	Revelation
2	Knowledge of mysteries	2	Knowledge	17	Word of instruction
3	Faith	6	Prophecy	8	Tongue
14	Give all I possess	11	Teaching	9	Interpretation
15	Surrender my body				

Table 1. The gifts of the Spirit in First Corinthians[38]

Never be content with the status quo. To taste of God's power just once is transformational. Give the Lord no peace, "Sue him for it" as the puritans would say of the sealing of the Holy Spirit. But

38. Fee, *Corinthians*, 212.

remember, the possession of these God given gifts doesn't mean the proverbial "hill of beans" if it is not matched with integrity. John Stott had some wise words on this:

> I confess to being frightened by the contemporary evangelical hunger for power, even the quest for the power of the Holy Spirit. Why do we want to receive power? Is it honestly power for witness (as in Acts 1:8), or power for holiness, or power for humble service? Or is it really a mask for personal ambition, a craving to boost our own ego, to minister to our self-importance, to impress, to dominate or to manipulate.[39]

Strive to possess gifts but equally, strive to possess integrity, then perhaps you will possess the greatest gift, to be like Christ.

---

39. Stott, *Calling Christian Leaders*, 41.

The Importance of Developing a Strong Character

MINISTERS HAVE LONG LOST the privilege of being listened to and respected simply because of their position. But only when they possess the trinity of integrity, gifting, and strength of character will a pastor have earned the right to be trusted. I have just written about integrity and gifts, and no one should argue against its importance in the life of any Christian, let alone a pastor. But you may be questioning the need for a subsequent chapter on developing strength of character. Surely, aren't integrity and strength of character the same thing? They are closely related I grant you and may not always be easy to separate but, no, they are not the same thing.

Consider this situation. You are travelling on a bus, and you observe a woman from the subcontinent with a red dot on her forehead, obviously a Hindu, and then you later see that she is being racially and religiously abused by another passenger. You may pat yourself on the shoulder and congratulate yourself that you did not join in because you knew such behavior was wrong, even if you did not particularly like the Hindu religion. This might be described as acting with integrity. But to act with character is to get up from your seat and protect the woman even though you will be accosted, and not necessarily just verbally. Character is more about the actions that should flow from possessing integrity; it is doing something about it. Often, that "something" will not be popular. Yet getting up from your seat should not be anything remarkable for someone who takes the words of Jesus seriously as he said, "Treat people the same way you want them to treat you" (Luke 6:31).

Be this man!

The well-known image in Figure 2 illustrates what strength of character is. It is thought to show a certain August Landmesser who, in 1936, refused to give a Nazi salute but instead sat with his arms crossed. His conviction cost him dearly. This chapter is primarily an encouragement to be that man. Increasingly, in the western world, we live in an environment that is hostile to the Christian gospel and Christian values. Consequently, it is taking evermore courage to stand out from the crowd and popular opinion. Paul wrote to the Corinthian church about how they should conduct themselves saying, "for we have regard for what is honorable, not only in the sight of the Lord, but also in the sight of other people" (2 Cor 8:21). Increasingly, our core Christian beliefs and the conduct that arises from them have become an anathema in the sight of other people. There can be no middle position of compromise on many matters.

People with strength of character will attempt to align their integrity with their personal convictions and be prepared to stand alone against the world. They will not base their actions on convenience and what benefits them personally or even on the latest trend but do what they believe is right. And they will do this simply because they believe it to be right! The cost may well be weighed but it is not the deciding factor and, as a result, they ought not easily surrender. A person can stand alone against the world on a clear gospel matter when they comprehend the reality that that they stand with this world's creator, Lord, and eventual judge.

An outstanding example of this is William Wilberforce (1798–1833) and his fight against the evils of slavery. It was a cause he could easily have surrendered due to the fierce opposition and lack of progress over many years. Yet still he stood alone, yet not alone. I could do better than to copy what is written on his memorial in Westminster Abby:

> In an age and country fertile in great and good men, he was among the foremost of those who fixed the character of their times; because to high and various talents, to warm benevolence, and to universal candor, he added the abiding eloquence of a Christian life. Eminent as he was in every department of public labor, and a leader in every work of charity, whether to relieve the temporal or the spiritual wants of his fellow-men, his name will ever be specially identified with those exertions which, by the blessing of god, removed from England the guilt of the African slave trade, and prepared the way for the abolition of slavery in every colony of the empire: in the prosecution of these objects he relied, not in vain, on god; but in the progress he was called to endure great obloquy and great opposition: he outlived, however, all enmity; and in the evening of his days, withdrew from public life and public observation to the bosom of his family. Yet he died not unnoticed or forgotten by his country: the peers and commons of England, with the Lord Chancellor and the Speaker at their head, in solemn procession from their respective houses, carried him to his fitting place among the mighty dead around, here to repose: till, through the merits of Jesus Christ, his only redeemer and saviour,

(whom, in his life and in his writings he had desired to glorify,) he shall rise in the resurrection of the just.[1]

August Landmesser was only a shipyard worker, one of the led, so there was not a great deal he could do to change things in such turbulent times other than set an example. However, a pastor is called and entrusted to lead. As Wilberforce became the conscience of a nation, so the pastor must be the conscience of those he/she leads. Of course, the congregation is responsible individually and all have the Holy Spirit to guide them yet there is an added dimension of being the shepherd of their soul and having a life that clearly mirrors Christ's. He/she can only do this if, as a leader, he/she possesses integrity with its associated quality of honesty but also, in equal measure, character and the commitment to action which is character's natural partner. Only such a person can inspire trust and loyalty in the congregation they serve and lead and, beyond that, spread influence into the wider church and secular community. While the acquisition of character should be and must be a work of grace, it also requires a willing and teachable heart as much as gaining integrity does.

However, we must not equate being steadfast in the face of adversity and opposition with character. It may well be and hopefully is, but it could also be no more than downright pigheadedness! I remember hearing in a tape of a sermon by Dr. Martin Lloyd Jones where he recounted a prayer he had heard from an old Presbyterian farmer. It went, "Lord may I always be right, for thou knowest I am hard to turn." Yet how true this is of many who lead, they just don't have the honesty to admit it. Instead, the character that should come from following Christ is built on possessing a teachable spirit and can change direction when incorrect actions and attitudes are exposed to the Spirit's gaze.

A church should not be just a holy huddle where the members keep each other warm against the icy blasts coming from a secular world. Too many faith communities are concerned only

1. Westminster Abby, https://www.westminster-abbey.org/abbey-commem orations/commemorations/william-wilberforce-family#:~:text=William%20 Wilberforce%20was%20buried%20in%20the%20north%20transept,The%20 family%20had%20long%20been%20settled%20in%20Yorkshire. par 3.

with keeping the integrity of the believers through rooting out any evil that is in the midst. Protecting and encouraging each other and striving for Christlikeness is a key role for pastor and church member alike but it is far from the full story. The church should also be looking outward and confronting the evil of this world that has set a course of abandoning every Christian value and celebrates every "victory" as liberation. I am not confusing a Christianized society with a Christian one. I am acknowledging that our world now praises evil as good and condemns good as evil but does so at great harm to itself. If we do not expose what is truly evil, then who will? Sadly, too often it is not the church, as some sectors have proven equally complicit in this world's glorification of sin. The true measure of character is how this is done. Our Heavenly Father loved this sinful world so much that when it was hopelessly lost, he sent his son to die for it. Jesus was the only friend sinners had and he still only saves sinners. When a pastor or a congregation has lost its love of sinners, whatever strength of character it may think it has, its opinions and its actions will be sadly askew.

Still, in this evil and corrupt world the pastor must have strong personal convictions and his/her decisions must be based on those convictions. It is difficult to see how without them he/she would have a sense of purpose sufficiently strong to stand with Jesus in the face of opposition. But more than that, without it such people cannot inspire their flock to add strength of character to what might be completely orthodox integrity and belief. Christianity must be concerned about honesty, commitment, and trustworthiness but it can still, at the same time, avert its eyes to the suffering in this world and so avoid taking a stand. Many did so with the evils of slavery, slums, and child labor. Many still do.

As with integrity, there is no *Dummies Guide to Gaining Strength of Character*. If your faith is worth anything, it will have action motivated by integrity at its core. As James, the brother of our Lord said, "Pure and undefiled religion in the sight of our God and Father is this: to visit orphans and widows in their distress, and to keep oneself unstained by the world" (Jas 1:26). True religion acts in the face of suffering. It is hard to comprehend how it would be possible for someone who has worked on strengthening their

PASTOR SERVED AL DENTE

character to not find a cause that they feel passionate enough to act consistently on. More to the point, it would seem unusual that a divinely implanted burden for action given to a pastor would not find willing co-workers among the congregation. Conversely, a pastor should be equally sensitive to the call to action that has made his/her congregation unique over what may even be generations. This should be nurtured and developed even further. (This subject is explored further in the chapter, *Compassion for the Weak*.)

It is not hard to find a wrong that needs the light, love, and mercy of the gospel to shine upon it. In this world of plenty there are people who are starving and, among noble words spoken about freedom, children are bought and sold into slavery. Whatever the cause, there must be something which aligns with gospel values that you feel deeply enough, and your church feels deeply enough, to do something about. Neither you nor your church will save the world and the Good Lord does not expect you to. But he does expect you to make a difference. Find a cause, or better still, allow him to lead you and impress upon your heart and the heart of your church, a cause. How far have you progressed along this path? Ask yourself this question, "On your passing, apart from your immediate family, who will weep"? And perhaps an equally piercing question is, "Who will rejoice?"

Someone Who Forgives

Be kind to one another, compassionate, forgiving each other,
just as God in Christ also has forgiven you.

—Eph 4:32

Years ago, one of our employees died of cancer. It was not a nice end for him. Another of our employees moonlighted as the local grave digger. It was hard work with a shovel and crowbar in a time before backhoes did the same thing in air-conditioned comfort. Our company provided a wreath, and we asked our employees if they would like to contribute $2 for a second wreath from his work-mates, (it was a while ago). Of course they did. But Reuben was six feet down a hole, so we didn't get the opportunity to ask him. When he checked his pay slip and saw that a small sum had been deducted for the wreath, he hit the roof. "He wronged me years ago and there is no way I will give $2 for his wreath," he protested along with a few choice expletives. I would have thought getting down deep and dirty and well paid digging his protagonist's hole was a suitable place to end hostility, but no, wrongs were to be savored and mulled over and revenge was sweet. Forgiveness was for others.

Likewise, churches can be a hotbed of unforgiveness with members not talking to each other and let's be perfectly honest, some members can be hard to love and even harder to forgive with-out help from above. Not surprisingly, resentments spill outside of the walls of the church to those who do not claim to know the for-giveness of Christ. (Nor are they likely to know it when the church is not a community of the forgiven and forgiving.) Yet, the paradox is that these same unforgiving members claim to take great comfort in the knowledge that God has forgiven them a debt so great that it could only be paid by Jesus being nailed to the cross.

Depending on your church tradition, how the assurance of this forgiveness is communicated varies, but in all, the minister has a crucial part. Consider the mechanics of this role across the different denominational groupings. In the Catholic Church where confession is a sacrament, forgiveness can only be given by a priest after confession and absolution. The Lutheran Church in Australia still recognizes private confession, but the normal practice is that there is a general confession of sin in the liturgy with absolution given by the pastor. He uses words like, "Christ gave the church the authority to forgive the sins of those who repent, and to declare to those who not repent that their sins are not forgiven. Therefore, upon your confession, I, as a called and ordained servant of the word announce the grace of God to all of you, and on behalf of my Lord Jesus Christ I forgive you all your sins, in the name of the Father and of the Son and the Holy Spirit." In my own Baptist practice, our pastors should have taught us and kept reminding us to keep a short account with our Lord, and as our own priest, regularly seek his forgiveness.

The sad reality is that a pastor can be diligent in the "business" of forgiveness between the congregation and their God and yet neglect the forgiveness that is necessary between the pastor himself/herself and his/her congregation. Why start with the pastor when the condition may be rampant among the members and may be where the real problem lies? Because the church should learn to forgive by watching their pastor forgive. Pastors and ministers need to forgive people no matter what they've done or said. I have seen members do despicable things to their pastor, lie to those in the church, smear them in the community, and attempt to destroy their reputation. A congregation can only know what true forgiveness is when, in the face of this, they see the minister return grace, mercy, compassion, love, and above all forgiveness.

The Christian community is meant to be one built on new relationships based on love, and that is not natural affection, but the very unnatural love that chooses to love (*agape*). It is also meant to be built on serving one another and considering the needs of others above our own. It is meant to be a community that lives by forgiveness, not without discipline,[1] but one where even this is aimed at forgiveness (2 Cor 2:5–8). Unfortunately, discipline without love is much easier as something is seen to be done that meets the expectation of those who have been forgiven little and forgive little.

To forgive is the most God-like thing we can do as our opening words to this chapter say. Yet even that sells it short. I am often drawn to the profound words of Gregory of Nyssa when talking about the radical nature of Christian forgiveness in the Lord's Prayer. He said, "Jesus wants your disposition to be a good example to God. We invite God to imitate us. Do thou the same as I have done. Imitate thy servant O Lord. Though he be only a poor beggar and thou art the King of the universe. I have shown great mercy to my neighbour imitate thy servant's charity."[2] Forgiven people cannot but help to forgive. Of all people who should never carry a grudge, it is the minister.

The pastor who will not forgive ultimately does not believe the Gospel. Consider, when our Lord walked this earth, our and his Father let ungodly men do whatever their dark, vile hearts could muster without restraint. Yet, in all of this Jesus could still say, "Father, forgive them; for they do not know what they are doing" (Luke 23:34). A pastor must be aware of the vast chasm that separated a sinful world, and that includes himself, from a holy God and the enormity of the cost to bridge that gap. If the gospel is understood, a pastor can't but realize how little is asked of him/her compared to the one who is said to be served and on whom they model their life. If you will not forgive, it is highly unlikely that you have been forgiven. You are like the unforgiving servant of Matthew 18:21–35. The verse in the Lord's Prayer that Gregory of Nyssa was referring to also has the negative side, "And forgive us our debts, as we also have forgiven our debtors," (Matt 6:12). Dare we, as unforgiving beggars, ask the King of the universe to imitate us?

1. Thielicke, *Ethics of Sex*, 243.
2. Barclay, *Lord's Prayer*, 95.

I am not naïve. There are things that are likely never to be resolved this side of the pearly gates. But never take consolation in being the one that was wronged, and you will be wronged and maligned if you follow Jesus closely. The initiative for forgiveness must never be dependent on the right response of the other. Forgiveness does not require an apology, nor should it be expected. Unforgiveness in a pastor is so serious that it disqualifies that person from ministry (and a layman from worship). Jesus said, "[23] Therefore, if you are presenting your offering at the altar, and there you remember that your brother has something against you, [24] leave your offering there before the altar and go; first be reconciled to your brother, and then come and present your offering" (Matt 5:23–24). Forgiveness, with accompanying works, is completely in your hands.

Preaching to the Heart not the Head

Your wickedness makes you as it were heavy as lead, and to
tend downwards with great weight and pressure towards hell;
and if God should let you go, you would immediately sink and
swiftly descend and plunge into the bottomless gulf, and your
healthy constitution, and your own care and prudence, and
best contrivance, and all your righteousness, would have no
more influence to uphold you and keep you out of hell, than a
spider's web would have to stop a falling rock. Were it not for
the sovereign pleasure of God, the earth would not bear you
one moment; for you are a burden to it; the creation groans
with you; the creature is made subject to the bondage of your
corruption, not willingly; the sun does not willingly shine
upon you to give you light to serve sin and Satan; the earth
does not willingly yield her increase to satisfy your lusts; nor
is it willingly a stage for your wickedness to be acted upon;
the air does not willingly serve you for breath to maintain the
flame of life in your vitals, while you spend your life in the
service of God's enemies.

—Jonathan Edwards, "Sinners in the Hands of an Angry God"

Back in the dark ages when I went to school, we had to learn
poems off by heart, the concept of which I suspect is a foreign
country to modern English students. Further, in grade eight, we

were introduced to prose and had to start memorizing it as well. A passage set for us one day was the words that introduce this chapter. Why our teacher should have chosen this passage I have no idea because he did not appear to have a spiritual bone in his body. It is drawn from a very famous sermon, *Sinners in the Hands of an Angry God,* preached by Jonathan Edwards, one of the leaders of the Great Awakening (peaked between 1740–42) and who became its theologian.[1] Perhaps it was simply because it is a great collection of words and ideas. The Great Awakening was the time of George Whitfield and the Wesley's and, unlike previous revivals, this was national in scope and explosive in its intensity.[2] The deadness of the church in the American colonies was driven by the increasing wealth and prosperity of the colonists, the influence of the rationalism of the Enlightenment and partly due to the simple fact that many of the pastors had not been converted themselves. Many considered it sufficient for the minister to know the doctrine without being affected by it.[3]

Even back then I was already aware of who Jonathan Edwards was. We learnt about him during Sunday school at the Congregational Church in my town. He was definitely the poster boy of our denomination. And yet, I look back and wonder how he could have been held in such reverence in a setting that had no place for the extraordinary outbursts of emotion that accompanied the conviction of sin, nor for his theology of a savior for sinners. Surely this is too harsh a description of a denomination where godly men were still serving? Sadly no. Stuart Piggin, the Australian church historian tells the story of how a Sydney Anglican minister Alan Whitham was travelling home in a train with Ivan Stebbins, then an old man but who had been chairman of the Congregational Union between 1943–4. Alan was bemoaning the decline in interest in doctrine:

---

1. His books, *Distinguishing Marks of a Work of the Spirit of God, A Faithful Narrative of the Surprising Works of God* and, *An account of the Revival of Religion in Northampton in 1740–1742* should be read by everyone praying for revival.

2. Edwards, "Sinners in the Hands of an Angry God," 13.

3. Marsden, *Jonathan Edwards,* 210–11.

Old Ivan was looking out the window and when he turned to look at me, there was a tear on his cheeks. He said, 'I killed the Congregational Church.' He explained that in the 1930s a committee of which he was chairman sent seven of their best students for the ministry to Germany for theological training and when they returned, they were all liberals. They destroyed the church.[4]

Isaac Watts, the English hymnwriter said of Edwards' sermon, "A most terrible (terrifying using the eighteenth century understanding of the word) sermon, which should have had a word of gospel at the end, though I think 'tis all true."[5] Edwards' liberal descendants in Australia would have said "terrible" in the modern sense of the word. The printed version of his sermon would have taken me one and a quarter hours to preach![6] Yet how much of it was actually preached that day and how much of an impact the famous (or infamous depending on your viewpoint) sermon had in the outbreak of revival in Enfield in New England is a matter for discussion. The reverend Stephen Williams from a nearby town described that day saying:

> Went over to Enfield, where we met dear Mr. Edwards of Northampton, who preached a most awakening sermon from those words, Deut. 32:35, and before the sermon was done there was a great moaning and crying out through the whole house—"What shall I do to be saved?" "Oh, I am going to hell!" "Oh what shall I do for a Christ?" and so forth— so that the minister was obliged to desist. [The] shrieks and cries were piercing and amazing. After some time of waiting, the congregation were still, so that a prayer was made by Mr. Wheelock, and after that we descended from the pulpit and discoursed with the people, some in one place and some in another. And amazing and astonishing: the power [of] God was seen and several souls were hopefully wrought upon that night, and oh the cheerfulness and pleasantness of their

4. Piggin, *Spirit, Word and World*, 93–4.
5. Edwards, "Sinners in the Hands of an Angry God," ix.
6. 7130 words at 100 words per minute.

countenances that received comfort. Oh that God would strengthen and confirm [their new faith]! We sang a hymn and prayed and dispersed the assembly.[7]

Truly, would we be comfortable with such pandemonium in our churches? Quickly, many of us would be reminding the poor pastor that everything should be done decently and in order as this is what our Lord wants. How many of us would be more content with the order of a church where the minister's heart has been little transformed by the gospel and whose messages may touch the emotions but never touch the heart. The seven Congregational liberals who destroyed their denomination had no eternal message of salvation, forgiveness, mercy, help, and encouragement in this life. Nor of a grave that has been sanctified by Christ's presence and eventual resurrection to a life in full fellowship with our maker.

Even in my "new" country of Australia you eventually run out of land and the families of New England were no different. What do you do with your second or third son when the army or the law was not an option? Many of them moved to a locality in Upstate New York between Lake Ontario and the Adirondacks. While there were individuals, it was more a movement of communities as pioneers preferred to purchase land from someone they knew from home, even at times former neighbors and to forge a new life near acquaintances.[8] They brought with them their heritage of revival and the rejection of the Half-way Covenant where children of church members could also become limited members[9] without any evidence of conversion. It was written about men in this district between 1795–1825:

> He was perhaps not himself a convert, though he had always gone to church and had scarcely considered doing otherwise. He awaited the day when the Holy Spirit would marvelously elect him to church membership. In

---

7. Edwards, "Sinners in the Hands of an Angry God," 2.

8. Cross, *Burned Over District*, 5–6.

9. These members were allowed to have their children baptised but were not allowed to have communion or vote on church business until they professed conversion.

the new country he might temporarily violate the Sab-
bath, swear, or drink too heavily, but he always expected
another revival to change his ways. His adolescent mind
readily leant itself to religious excitement. He probably
married a "professing" Christian, who constantly warned
him of his dangerous position, and certainly intended to
rear a family of respectable, churchgoing Christians.[10]

Their ministers, in the Calvinist tradition, could only warn
them of the miseries of Hell. He might prepare them, so they were
in a position to receive grace through encouraging them to strive
fervently to keep God's Law. However, only when they realized they
could not keep the Law would they be truly prepared for grace. As
one historian wrote. "As their unconverted hearers were destitute
of faith, had no efficient belief in the word of God, it was evidently
impossible to subdue them with proof-texts and expositions of
scripture."[11] Then into an expectant and "prepared" population of
Upstate New York broke former lawyer and now Presbyterian minister Charles Finney (1792–1875) with his "new measures" declar-
ing that man had free-will to choose. It was recorded:

> At Evans Mills, he was troubled that the congregations
> continuously said they were "pleased" with his sermons.
> He set about to make his message less pleasing and more
> productive. At the end of his sermon, which stressed the
> need for conversion, he took a bold step: "You who have
> made up your minds to become Christians, and will give
> your pledge to make your peace with God immediately,
> should rise up.
>
> The entire congregation, having never heard such a
> challenge, remained in their seats. "You have taken your
> stand," he said. "You have rejected Christ and his gospel."
> The congregation was dismissed, and many left angry.
>
> The next evening, Finney preached on wickedness,
> his voice like "a fire . . . a hammer . . . [and] a sword."
> But he offered no chance to respond. The next night, the
> entire town turned out, including a man so angry with
> Finney that he brought a gun and intended to kill the

10. Cross, *Burned Over District*, 8.

11. Tracey, *Great Awakening*, 4.

evangelist. But that night, Finney again offered congregants a chance to publicly declare their faith. The church erupted—dozens stood up to give their pledge, while others fell down, groaned, and bellowed. The evangelist continued to speak for several nights, visiting the new converts at their homes and on the streets.[12]

From 1825–35 revivals followed his preaching which was often extemporaneous and with the style of a lawyer arguing his case. Finney became one of the leaders of the Second Great Awakening and that locality was so engulfed by waves of revival that it became known as the "burnt over district." Finney would pave the way for evangelists that touched the world including Dwight L. Moody, Billy Sunday, and Billy Graham.

Though diametrically opposed in their preaching. I suspect that Edwards and Finney would barely recognize much of what passes for preaching now in the west. How little of it touches the heart. W.G. Taylor (1845–1934) was a Methodist evangelist working in Queensland who saw remarkable revivals in locations close to my home. He said in the 1920's:

> The other day I was chatting with one of our most popular preachers on the distressing problem of our empty down-town church. I ventured upon the old man's argument and referred to the full churches of a quarter of a century ago. The answer came swiftly and fiery, "The world has all altered since then. We are breathing an entirely different atmosphere. Men are not to be reached today as they were reached two or three decades ago." I do not believe a word of it. It is the changed atmosphere within, and not outside the Church, that explains our failure. It does not require that a man should be a keen student of Church history to be set to rest upon that point . . . Try as I may, I cannot rid myself of the feeling that it is the Church of God that is largely to blame for much of the present neglect of religion, the forgetfulness of God, the ignoring of his laws, everywhere so patent to us all.[13]

12. Christianity Today, "Charles Finney," par 8–11.
13. Taylor, *Pathfinders*, 67.

Old Ivan wept as he thought of the destruction he had caused by rejecting the heritage of great, and contemporary for him, Australian Congregational evangelists such as Lionel Fletcher (1877–1954). Instead, he chose the "enlightened" path of eviscerated Christianity of German liberalism. Their new message emptied a once vibrant denomination because it couldn't touch the heart. I realize that few of my readers will be tempted to take that path. More seductive is the attraction of a degraded Christianity. This form of Christianity is intended not to be offensive to a world that has rejected the need of a savior and finds the validity of even a very diminished understanding of Jesus as a moral teacher an abomination. Such a Christianity will walk the tightrope of complying with anti-scriptural legislation from secular government while attempting to remain "Christian." The message of the cross is offensive to the sinner and if you are preaching to the heart, you will and must offend and be offensive to some. Peace with a sinful and lost world does not come with peace with God. My old mentor told me how, after funerals, one of our local prominent "sinners" would always say to him, "You bastard Liebeldt. You always get under a man's skin." Likewise, your preaching should annoy or anger, but hopefully with God's grace, also convict and convert. Both Peter and Stephen were filled with the Spirit, and both preached to the heart, but the results were very different (Acts 2:37; 7:54).

Jonathan Edwards and Charles Finney were fortunate to see revival. I have not known times like that though sometimes I think my preaching does touch the heart though not as often as I would like.[14] Once, and only once, I was permitted to go further and break through this into the spiritual realm where I touched the divine when preaching. I can think of no other way to describe it, and it deeply affected the hearts of the hearers and frightened me. People outside the room asked, "What happened in there?" What of you? For most it would have been the "day of small things" (Zec 4:10). Enough blessing for the Lord to remind you that he is still close by but apparently little more. The Lord in his wisdom has told us to be thankful for even those days but we have come to believe that

14. A book of my sermons, *Sermons from a Potato Field,* has been published by Wipf and Stock.

this is the way it always has been and accept that it always must be. And what of your preaching? What do you do for every Sunday of your ministry when men and women will not cry out for someone to lead them to a gracious savior? How different to the day of Pentecost and the first sermon preached, "When the people heard this, they were cut to the heart and said to Peter and the other apostles, "Brothers, what shall we do?" (Acts 2:37).

Preaching to the heart is not entertainment, though it can contain humor; nor is it simply informing the mind, though it must, nor is it bypassing the intellect and just stirring the emotions. The word used in Acts 2:27 is *kardia* but it is one of those words whose precise meaning is hard to pin down to just one English word and it does change with the context. Briefly, it could be summarized as the center and source of the whole inner life, including its thinking, feeling, and choosing. As such the main function of preaching to the heart is not to inform. Its primary purpose is to transform. This is ultimately the work of God yet there is at its core a human aspect. The biblical usage of *heart* is clearly seen in the way it is contrasted to outward actions such as, "This people honors Me with their lips, but their heart is far away from Me" (Matt 15:8). Similarly in the Old Testament, "Do not look at his appearance or at the height of his stature, because I have rejected him; for God does not see as man sees, since man looks at the outward appearance, but the Lord looks at the heart" (1 Sam 16:7). Preaching to the heart is intended to change the inner life of a person as it targets who and what they are and should not leave the hearers apathetic.

The first thing you must do is master your calling, as this is something you have full control over. Being a good preacher does not happen by accident. So much of a minister's work is spoken, and speaking well is a skill you can and must develop. As Paul reminded Timothy, "fan into flame the gift of God, which is in you" (2 Tim 1:6). And it was a reminder rather than something new to him. We can so easily let things slide, some blessings, some favorable comments and we are in danger of thinking we have arrived. The reminder needs to come to us all as with Timothy, to fan the gift into flame. Julius Caesar was very busy conquering the world, butchering untold thousands, and upending the political system of

Rome. Yet, in all this he took time off to travel to Rhodes and learn rhetoric.[15] If you want to sway an army, a mob, or a senate, knowing how to speak well is essential and he was already acknowledged as a good speaker at that time, yet he understood the need to excel. So must you, as good content needs good delivery.

You may question whether prayer, not mastering your calling is the first thing, but I would argue that mastering your craft and having to think deeply about spiritual things is prayer when it is driven by love of our redeemer.[16] To do this is an acknowledgement of the very seriousness of the call to allow God to speak through you by expounding his word. Your understanding of the seriousness of your call will develop and you will become bold in the content of your sermons. Hugh Latimer (1487–1555) once preached in Westminster Abbey when Henry VIII was in the congregation. In the pulpit he said to himself, "Latimer! Latimer! Latimer! Be careful what you say. The king of England is here!" Then he went on, "Latimer! Latimer! Latimer! Be careful what you say. The King of Kings is here." Woe to us if we cower before Mrs. Smith.

Paul rejected Greek philosophy and rhetoric and the tricks and embellishments that went with it as the means of spreading the gospel, powerful and entertaining as they may have been in his setting (1 Cor 1:17). It is not the same thing as saying we do not have to preach well. As a student in Florida, Billy Graham first preached from sermon outlines of great preachers to the alligators and birds and if all else failed to "a congregation of cypress stumps that could neither slither nor fly away." Later he would use empty churches.[17] You don't have to have an audience to practice. By contrast, not too long before I wrote these words, we had a third-year theological student visit our church and he delivered his first sermon! I fear it was not far short of a persecution of the saints.

There are ways of learning the art of your calling. My bishop friend insists that ministers join Toastmasters. At my own college,

15. Meier, *Julius Caesar*, 104.

16. Loosely paraphrasing Thomas Aquinas, "I receive Thee ransom of my soul. For love of Thee have I studied and kept vigil toiled preached and taught . . ." Catholics, "St. Thomas Aquinas," par 26.

17. Graham, *Just as I am*, 49, 58.

we had to study speech and drama. Above all, practice, practice, practice. A recently ordained Lutheran pastor informed me how, in his studies, the lectures in many of the subjects all focused on application in preaching. Colleges which only produce academics who cannot touch the heart have no place in the church. They will do more harm than good, and such ministers and churches exist.

Occasionally, I would have opportunity to visit the local Lutheran church where my mentor was pastor. I have visions of him standing beside the pulpit, with his left arm resting on it and speaking without notes to the congregation. And it was more speaking than sermonizing and yet he would touch hearts deeply. He told me about the first time he preached in a church when he was in seminary. He delivered a children's address first and then the sermon and he admitted that he floundered. His homiletics lecturer was a member of the church, and he took him aside and told him, "Next time, make your children's address the sermon and dumb down your children's talk and you will be all right." He accepted this advice, and God blessed it. He told me he did not have to do much counselling as God did most of it through his preaching. The simplicity of his sermons belied the depth of study that undergirded them. When he eventually retired and left town, a removalist came for his belongings. A second removalist came for his books. A pastor who has not studied deeply, when he has had the opportunity, is likely to do more harm than good.

Some years back when traveling through Stradbroke in the UK, my friend took me in to see All Saints Church. This was the church of J. C. Ryle (1816–1900), a leading Anglican evangelical in a different age. During his time in Stradbroke, he had the church renovated and "redecorated." As you stand in his old pulpit you can see texts he had written on the cross beams of the roof. They start off, "God be merciful to me a sinner," then "I will arise and go to my father," then, "Create in me a clean heart O God," then "Search the scriptures, prove all things," and finally, "Believe in the Lord Jesus Christ and thou shalt be saved." It was a reminder that a minister must have tasted the mercy and grace of the judge of the living and the dead. Likewise, if we have not experienced that same grace and know the certainty of it, then woe is us. Without it, what word do we have to preach and what word can our lives express? It certainly won't be, "Be reconciled to God."

From where the congregation sat, they saw different verses and they described what should be the response of all who hear the word of grace preached to the heart. These were, "Strive to enter in at the strait gate," "We have redemption through his blood," and finally, "We have an advocate with the father." For those who hear the word, the command is to move from the illusions that may have satisfied to the substance of reconciliation with the judge of the living and the dead. Carved deep in the pulpit are the words, "Woe is me if I preach not the gospel." Woe to the seven liberal Congregationalists who preached a different gospel. Woe to us if the gospel does not consume our heart. Woe to the minister if he/she does not fan the desire to preach until it develops into something that is almost overwhelming.

A long time ago, I studied at Elim Bible College in the UK. George Jeffreys (1889–1962) who founded the Elim denomination was a convert of the Welsh revival. After I returned to Australia, someone played me some old 78 RPM recordings of him preaching. What I remember of them is that every word, all of which was weighed and considered, cut you to the heart, even coming through a scratchy old shellac record. This is something you cannot learn as it goes beyond mastering the technicality of speaking. Rather, it is a gift of God, one that you must earnestly seek and give the Lord no peace till you receive it. To go beyond even this and to touch heaven once will make you realize how far short your preaching is from what it could be. Increasingly I have been asking my Lord, "Once more."

Now reader, you may accuse me also of going down the old man's argument of longing for the old days that will never return. Not a bit of it. Those days never left this world. If you made this accusation, it would be just an admission that you have let your limited Christian experience be the arbiter of what you expect Christian life always to be. We should not judge the lax state of the church in the west as representing the state of the church worldwide. I have been blessed to see the life of the church and its hunger for God's word in some parts of the developing world. There is nothing like an "Amen" or "Thank you Jesus." in response to your preaching to give it life. A few years back, I spoke at a conference in the hills of Southern Mindanao, terrorist country. We travelled to the site in Manny Pacquiao's Toyota tray top (no one was going to touch that) and were guarded at night with machine guns yet, here, we had trouble getting people to attend church in a pandemic even when guidelines permitted! I was told to prepare a three-hour sermon for that conference as the organizer told me about the expectations of the listeners. They will tell him, "We have walked three hours to get here, and you only preach for an hour and a half, it is not fair pastor."

The big question for a western preacher is the same as that asked of Ezekiel, "Can these dry bones live?" Yet, a more pertinent (or impertinent) question would be, can your dry bones live? We can take no better advice than that given to John Wesley, and which changed the direction of world history:

> Saturday, March 4. —I found my brother at Oxford, recovering from his pleurisy; and with him Peter Bohler; by whom, in the hand of the great God, I was, on Sunday, the fifth, clearly convinced of unbelief, of the want of that faith whereby alone we are saved.
>
> Immediately it struck into my mind, "Leave off preaching. How can you preach to others, who have not faith yourself?" I asked Bohler whether he thought I should leave it off or not. He answered, "By no means." I asked, "But what can I preach?" He said, "Preach faith till you have it; and then, because you have it, you will preach faith."
>
> Accordingly, Monday, 6, I began preaching this new doctrine, though my soul started back from the work. The first person to whom I offered salvation by faith alone was a prisoner under sentence of death. His name was Clifford. Peter Bohler had many times desired me to speak to him before. But I could not prevail on myself so to do; being still, as I had been many years, a zealous asserter of the impossibility of a deathbed repentance.[18]

18. Wesley, *Journal*, 58.

Where to from here? As an old pastor who did preach to the heart told me, the greatest advice he has for every preacher, young, old, experienced, inexperienced is to preach Jesus, preach the word and do it in the power of the Spirit. And I would add, as I have already mentioned, master your craft, and I repeat, good content needs good delivery. Do so until your preaching reaches another level. Further, as I also mentioned, give the Lord no peace until you are conscious of an anointing upon your preaching and then still not be satisfied. Like Wesley, you have a message for prisoners under sentence of death. They just don't know it. May your heart and the heart of your hearers be "strangely warmed."[19]

Yet still there is something beyond all this. I have spoken about how it is not enough for doctrine to be known, but that it must be believed. I have also spoken about how the Lord's strength is available to anoint the words you speak with power not of your own. By God's grace they have the power to create what was not there before. Beyond this, the truth of God's word is to be lived. It is to be lived by pastors who can say, "nevertheless" as they face the undeniable realities in which they find themselves. The realities which seem to be opposed to God and his benevolence. This is the truly scary bit. For many in the western world, the lives they have lived are sheltered with little experience of suffering. There is a depth to preaching that can only come through suffering and the dark night of the soul. That my friends is in the Good Lord's hands and never pray to go there.

19. Wesley, *Journal*, 64.

A Person of Undivided Attention

32 But I want you to be free from concern. One who is unmarried is concerned about the things of the Lord, how he may please the Lord; 33 but one who is married is concerned about the things of the world, how he may please his wife, 34 and his interests are divided. The woman who is unmarried, and the virgin, is concerned about the things of the Lord, that she may be holy both in body and spirit; but one who is married is concerned about the things of the world, how she may please her husband. 35 I say this for your own benefit, not to put a restraint on you, but to promote what is appropriate and to secure undistracted devotion to the Lord.

—1 COR 7:32–35

PERHAPS THE MOST ENIGMATIC person from Australia's convict past is the Rev. Samuel Marsden. Samuel's father had been a blacksmith but, at a young age, became an orphan. He was fortunate to be educated through charity but remained tough and country bred. Under the patronage of William Wilberforce, the great English reformer, Marsden arrived in the small convict settlement of Sydney in 1794. Though living in Paramatta, then the other major settlement, he was, for a time, the only minister in the penal settlement with responsibility also for Sydney. The "Christian" community was small and made up of soldiers and convicts who, in most cases, only attended services under compulsion. He wrote of his charges, "All the higher ranks are lost to God and Religion, and you may so form an idea of the character of the lower orders,"[1] While there were committed Christians, and his home became the center of the growing evangelical circle in the colony, he saw little reward for his efforts.

In 1809, there was a massacre in New Zealand (then known as Aotearoa) where seventy European sailors were killed and eaten at Whangaroa by the Māori. In response, Marsden founded the Philanthropic Society and along with three others attempted to cross "the ditch" and evangelize the Māori. Governor Macquarie forbade him, so he simply purchased a brig with his own money and, along with three laymen and some exiled Māori, set sail for New Zealand. The laymen had come from England when, on one of his visits, he tried to interest the Church Missionary Society in starting the Christian work on Aotearoa. Not entirely unsurprisingly, there were no takers among the ordained men for a career that appeared to be short lived and end as a victim of cannibalism. Marsden is credited with introducing Christianity to New Zealand and for organizing the evangelism of the South Pacific. On another occasion, an Australian convict who had come under conviction of his sinfulness tried to murder the parson by attempting to drown him. Marsden overcame the would-be murderer and, in the end, saved his life instead. Whereas most men would have dragged the convict to the authorities and then the gallows, the two instead became close friends.[2]

This all points to a man of exceptional virtue and courage and someone on whom to model a Christian life. But it is a fair question to ask, where does a child of charity get the money to purchase a brig? He took on a lot of extra work, some directly related to ministry such as the supervision of the government clothing factory where degraded women worked and whose spiritual care he took on. It was secular work nonetheless, but this was nothing compared to his appointment as a magistrate in 1795. In this role he has become infamous as the "flogging parson." He was eventually removed from office in 1822 because he imposed illegal sentences

1. Murray, *Australian Christian Life*, 30.
2. Murray, *Australian Christian Life*, 32–3.

and used his office to attack political opponents.[3] He was complicit and accepting of a system that was brutal and inhumane and the sentences handed out and the physical damage caused by the lash were horrendous beyond description. An historian of the 1850's described him this way:

> Nothing can be more opposite than the estimates of his character, given by the partisans of the emancipists, and those furnished by his ecclesiastical associates. Soured by the vices rampant around him, and perhaps deteriorated by the administration of justice, when it was hard to distinguish the magistrate from the executioner, he does not always appear to have merited the unmeasured eulogies of his friends . . . The servant, charged with a misdemeanor, he flogged; who then took to the bush, and reappearing, charged with a capital crime, was hanged; and the magisterial divine attended him on the scaffold.[4]

He saw the role of the law as suppressing iniquity. It was not the gospel and could not save men but provided a safe place to do mission work. While there were not many who could have been called on to fulfil the role of magistrate, nothing explains or excuses why his sentences were more severe.[5]

He also participated in the generous grants of land to free settlers which he augmented with further purchases of land and was credited as being "the best practical farmer in the country."[6] Marsden, along with his neighbor and arch enemy, John Macarthur,[7] were the first to see how important wool could be to the young colony. Marsden provided the first commercial shipment of wool and

---

3. Gladwin, "Flogging Parsons," 389. He illegally had a young Irish man tortured with 300 lashes of the cat of nine tails, unsuccessfully it turned out, to have him give up names of those involved in a revolution.

4. Allen, *Samuel Marsden*, par 34.

5. Piggin. *Fountain of Public Prosperity*, 91.

6. Murray, *Australian Christian Life*, 33.

7. Macarthur was a highly influential figure in the early British colonization of New South Wales. He started as an officer in the New South Wales Corps and became a racketeer, entrepreneur, grazier, rebellion leader and, politician.

saw himself instigating the commerce of this new colony.[8] While the provision of food was paramount in the early years of settlement "it was harder to justify with the passage of time. Marsden's extensive acquisitions of land for farming did not befit his calling as a Christian preacher."[9] Marsden could be described as a man of divided attention, who in his own words, believed that "God allows us plenty of time to attend to the concerns of this world, as well as to that which is to come."[10] He was a man with a foot planted firmly in each world. My comments earlier in this book about taking note of who rejoices on your death is very pertinent.

Consider the opposite example with Martin Luther. The former Augustinian friar had sworn an oath of poverty but suddenly had to provide for his wife, Käthe and their subsequent six children plus ten others. He only had a small stipend and received no income for lecturing at the university, yet he was very generous, pawning his possessions to give to the needy, trusting that God would allow him to repay.[11] His personal finances left him depressed. He lived in the old monastery, so they took in paying boarders along with their family. When a prince wanted to stay with him, the nobleman was warned that, "An odd assortment of young people, students, young girls, widows, old women and children lives in the Doctor's home; this makes for great disquiet in the house, and there are many who pity Luther because of it."[12]

But such an impoverished life was not necessary. Hans Lufft who published 100,000 of his German translation of the Bible became the third richest man in Wittenberg. Possibly as many as 900,000 extra were pirated by other publishers.[13] Yet Luther never took a fee for his translation, nor for any of his large body of works.[14] The monastery had brewing rights, so Käthe took them over and

---

8. Piggin. *Fountain of Public Prosperity*, 90.

9. Murray, *Australian Christian Life*, 34.

10. Marsden, *Sermon 24*, 16.

11. Friedenthal, *Luther*, 441, 443.

12. Friedenthal, *Luther*, 443.

13. Friedenthal, *Luther*, 312.

14. Metaxas, *Martin Luther*, 434.

used the brewery to their benefit. It appears she made quite a brew.[15] My Methodist mother and Rechabite[16] father would have said that it was better to take the royalties than be "a purveyor of alcoholic beverages." Luther also refused to engage a solicitor to draft his will. On his death, his "will" that would have cared for Kāthe, was found to be invalid and she was left destitute. When considering her fate, one of Luther's biographers noted, "When Luther's marriage to Kāthe is held up as the foundation of the evangelical parsonage and the model of family life, it is well to remember that the fate of evangelical pastors' widows down through the centuries can hardly be counted amongst the glorious achievements of the German ruling authorities who owed so much to Luther."[17]

The title of this chapter is *A Person of Undivided Attention* but is that really possible or even desirable? The colonial parson with his big house stood with one foot firmly entrenched in the world of heaven and the other far too soundly in the world of commerce. The reformer, for his part, had both his feet in and his focus on God's kingdom. If Samuel Marsden had not been successful commercially, he would not have been able to embark on the evangelism of the Māori by bypassing the need for the governor's permission. Had Luther considered his time and energy worthy of reward, (this surely is a biblical principle) and had he engaged a solicitor, his family, and particularly his widow, would have avoided much hardship.

In the chapter, *Gifting and Integrity*, I claimed that there are up to seventeen gifts of the Holy Spirit listed in First Corinthians but, of course, I left one out. What about the gift of chastity? Strangely, I have only heard one person pray for that which was a young lady I was keeping company with. (That was never going to be a long-term success was it!) Paul spoke about this gift in chapter seven but when it comes to this gift, I suspect most of my readers will feel sympathy for Augustine when he said, "Lord give me chastity and self-control—but not yet."[18] Most of us will take what the Apostle

---

15. Friedenthal, *Luther*, 440,

16. The Independent Order of Rechabites was founded in the UK in 1835 and Australia in 1843. It was a friendly society that promoted total abstinence.

17. Friedenthal, *Luther*, 447

18. Augustine, *Confessions*, 8.7.

saw as the second best course, that of marriage (1 Cor 7:38) and yet it is meant to bring with it blessings beyond measure. No, while the charge to be of "undivided attention" sounds good and spiritual it seems to me that it can be anything but. We live in a world where we have legitimate concerns, the more so if we are married and have a family. Misfortune due to circumstances beyond their control can overcome any family but misfortune originating from neglect to do what was prudent is an entirely different matter. How does a pastor find an acceptable balance, the more so if they must also work to provide a livelihood as well as serve?

When I was writing the chapter, *People that Listen*, I pulled down from my bookshelf Dietrich Bonhoeffer's book, *Life Together* and out dropped a picture of that girlfriend that had been there for almost fifty years! I was immediately filled with regret. It wasn't regret for not marrying her but with the realization that youth is definitely wasted on the young. It brought back memories of 1973 and the start of a friendship that had lasted for fifty years. The mother of the young lady in question had "second sight" and knew that her daughter was going to die in an accident when she was out with me! I don't know if there is an optometrist for people with second sight. It is not quite the same as double vision. We are both, to my knowledge, looking at the green side of the grass. We could only meet at her church, and it was a small Strict Baptist chapel in a small town, two and a half hours travel (but only twenty-two miles) from the Pentecostal college where I was studying. Such is love, especially in an English winter. As mentioned, my friendship with her was doomed but it was the start of a long friendship with that Baptist pastor and his family.

Some money had come through from Australia for my expenses and I normally sent a tenth to a certain person. I was conscious of a little voice inside me saying, "Hold off." I was staying at the home of this pastor one holiday, and I was again conscious of that little voice saying that this is where the gift was to go. My friend would bring up a cup of tea every morning, so I had put it on the bedside table for him to take. He tried very hard to get me to take it back, but I was just as firm in saying, "No," so he "reluctantly" took it. I learned later in the morning that their financial situation was so dire that they had set that day for the Lord to provide, or they would abandon full-time service. Their ministry had already been fruitful and would eventually bring many to faith.

My friend at the age of twenty-two was an accountant and was offered the position of Head of Data Processing for Europe for a large pharmaceutical company. This would have left the family financially comfortable. At the same time, he received a call from this small church in Surrey to be their full-time pastor. There were only fifteen members! The stipend was small but fortunately, there was a manse that supplemented his income. Still, even for 1967, the two combined were hopelessly inadequate. The call and the acceptance were both acts of faith, but it required that my friend take on part-time accountancy work for a period. Three years later, one of the partners at the practice where he worked died.

At the same time, my friend's father was also the pastor of a church but at only 55 years of age he was dying of a brain tumor. My friend declared war on God saying, "If you want pastors, you could have my dad, but if you didn't want my dad, he couldn't have me!" Later in that very same day, he was offered a partnership with the accountants. It came with a house and car and free time to keep the role as pastor. It was so attractive to have a foot firmly in both worlds and the draw was powerful after some very hard and mentally draining years but, ultimately, the Lord took first place. As my friend said, the Devil knows what buttons to push and when to push them. I only knew the church when it had probably the same fifteen members. However, there was a time before when a number were converted and left to study for and eventually go on to serve the Lord in ministry. The church went back to where it had been.

After nine years, my friend could have taken the pastorate of any large Strict Baptist (now known as Grace Baptist) church, but he accepted a call from a church in Suffolk with five active members! They were small in number but large in faith and had just built a modern manse beside the church. (That church incidentally was shaped like a coffin.) While the church made a faith commitment to pay him £750 per year, the total of the previous year's offering, again he had to work part-time as an accountant to provide for his family for a while. During over thirty-four years pastoring that church he saw many conversions and some mini revivals. He left the church with nearly ninety members.

He retired in 2010 and, like many more ministers before and after, they did not own a home. That is the danger of making the manse part of the salary package. In Australia, not owning your home in retirement brings with it the specter of a very difficult old age and it is not any different in the UK. My friend still works despite being almost eighty. He takes funerals, a ministry which has brought some to faith, but he works through necessity not choice. When speaking of his life, he said he had made "some grave mistakes" that made his retirement harder than it needed to be despite appearing to be good at the time. Inheritance money could have bought a home, but he acknowledges he lived with more ease and also spent money on missionary trips around the world. And make no mistake, these trips were blessed and the kingdom advanced.

His life was governed by the principle of putting his hand to the plough and not looking back and also of not joining the chorus of the world by chasing after possessions and seeking security in them instead of in the Lord. My old Congregational minister mentioned in the introduction was in the same situation, but he did not have a wife to support in retirement, so he lived with his sister. But when you choose to marry you cannot live and plan as though you were still single. It is necessary to plan for the others in your life ahead of your own concerns and even your own gift of faith. Under Saxon law, Luther's widow would have been left with only a chair and a distaff and only the intervention of the Elector saved her from this extreme situation.[19] What will be your spouse's situation on your death?

The position with the Baptist Union of Queensland is that the manse is not meant to be part of the salary package. The minister is expected to make plans to purchase a home when in ministry and this is wise. The danger, of course, is that the higher income will be spent unwisely. This is where denominational organizations can play a more direct role. In my opinion, retirement planning is where the wisdom of Solomon is needed. A minister must be of undivided

19. Friedenthal, *Luther*, 447

attention yet holding in tension a sufficient vision of this world so that the necessary prudence is given to the future beyond ministry. Marsden was wrong. The Lord does not give sufficient time to have feet firmly in both worlds. I know of a pastor and his family in the slums of Hyderabad who were living in a large cardboard box on a house roof. To the day he dies, he and his wife will be constantly pleading for their daily bread and a roof over their heads. What a blessing it is for most of us in the western world to have the opportunity to plan a future. It can be a very spiritual exercise.

,

A Person with Compassion
for the Weak

A bent reed He will not break off

And a dimly burning wick He will not extinguish;

He will faithfully bring forth justice.

—Isa 42:3

I HAD AN EMPLOYEE who was conscientious and did very good work, but his health had deteriorated to the point that I understood, very sadly, that his employment was no longer viable. The condition was such that he was not likely ever to get better, and the best thing was for him to return to his parents to see out his days in the care of those he loved and who loved him. Rightly or wrongly, letting an employee go is a minefield under Australian employment legislation. Part of this process was for him to be assessed by a doctor who specializes in workplace health to see if there was any possibility of remaining in employment. Shortly after, I had to see this same doctor also as I realized I was not far from having a breakdown myself and needed help. I say "doctor," but he didn't like to be called that as he saw it as a term now stripped of its full respect as he said his vet and his dentist and even the local chiropractors call themselves "doctors." (Apologies to any vet, dentist or chiropractor reading this.) He asked me, "Why are you a rescuer?" I replied, "Because the Good Lord rescued me." It should not be otherwise.

A wise man once said that the Good Lord has so many doctors that he must be sick! At least we can take some comfort in knowing that he is not "dead" as the young Congregational minister from the introduction thought. I know what a hard slog it is to achieve letters after your name. By the time someone has reached the dizzying heights of academia, they can run the risk of seeing themselves as the rescuer rather than the rescued. The old preacher and author, William Huntington (1745–1813) used to sign his name with the letters S.S. Everybody thought it was an academic achievement but eventually someone had the temerity to ask what they were all thinking, "What do the letters mean," as they did not know such a degree? He told them, "Sinner Saved." The foot of the cross is a leveler for men and woman, boys and girls, rich and poor, foreigner and native, ignorant and educated and, above all, for weak and strong. The beginning point in all our dealings with others is that we have been rescued and it is only God that can do the rescuing. Of course, we can and should self-improve, but the rescuing that lasts for eternity is God's work.

Bobby and Phill making a product for the author. Both had dreadful medical problems before they were ten years old.

I have been a Gideon for a long time and one of the things we did was to hand out New Testaments to first year students at our local university. Initially, Gideons were welcomed but with the changing tide of secularism eventually we were all but banned. I received a letter from the administration one year advising us that we risked an assault charge if we offered a Testament to a student! For many years also I found work at my premises for people with intellectual disabilities. Regularly, Bobby would say to me that he was sorry that he had not been to work but he had been sick. I hadn't twigged, but the supervisor eventually told me that Bobby did not understand what a weekend was. If you had not been to work, it could only be because you were sick! About the time I received the letter from some of the greatest minds in the country, Bobby told me that pastor told him that Jesus had a home in heaven, and you could see that he believed it. This man had had a stroke before he was ten and his brain was as withered as his hand, but he had the wisdom to grasp all that was necessary. I fear that too often fools of the caliber of those who wrote the "assault" letter are the subject of our efforts to the expense of those who in their simplicity have the child-like faith Jesus seeks.

Let me give you two more examples. A friend, a divorced and then single mother had a child who was intellectually disabled to the point that he could not talk. Up to his death in his twenties, he never said his mother's name or any other word, except once. Sometime when he was young, they were at a Bible study and, for some reason or other, his mother was out of the room. The minister asked the group, 'How can we be saved?" The boy answered clearly. 'By the Holy Spirit." He never spoke again! Another story closer to home, my grandmother, who had been a very godly woman, had a stroke and was in a coma for twelve years which she spent in a church run nursing home. One day, my dear Auntie was visiting her mother and the minister was also visiting that ward. She asked the minister to give her mother communion and he refused saying, 'It would mean nothing to her." Silly man for saying "No" to my auntie, you only do that once! She told him outright, "You will give my mother communion!" Again, he refused but handed the kit to my auntie and told her to do it herself and she was not backwards in coming forward. My grandmother had every appearance of having no awareness of anything and as auntie sat her up and put the bread and the wine to my grandmother's lips, she burst into tears. At the end of the bed, the minister was also in tears and begging for forgiveness. "I never knew, I never knew," he sobbed. My point is that there can be things going on under the surface that we have little comprehension of, and we make a grave mistake when we substitute intellectual assent for faith. They are not the same thing.

My mentor was described as "a special servant of the Lord . . . a ball of energy, filled with the Spirit and practical good sense and with a heart for sharing the love of Jesus." He told me that he put a question to the church he served, "Jesus ministered to the lepers, but we don't have any, what is the closest we have?" They recognized that for many in society at that time, an intellectually disabled child was the family shame and was hidden largely out of sight. These were our local "lepers" that needed to be served and loved. However, he could not carry this all on his own shoulders. So what happened so that a church would actually do something and move from lofty thoughts and actually take on ministry to this group? Leadership for a start. My old mentor had a brother with Down Syndrome that he was not ashamed of so I can understand why he would want to be involved in serving the disabled. Recently, I asked how he was able to get his church to follow. Back then the church was large and in a church of that size there would have already been a group of their own that needed help. And it was a time when there was a willing spirit to volunteer and minimal government regulations made it much easier to be involved. Importantly, I think the Good Lord hid from the congregation how big this small start would become.

How quickly any one of us can come crashing from the "pride of life" and become no more than a "bruised reed." I had another employee who was very skilled in operating one of my machines, but it appeared he only worked to enable his love for football, sex, and drinking. For years, I looked for a replacement and could not find anyone. Skills are not enough when workplace commitment and trust is lacking. I overheard him talking about the team of disabled workers I had on site, and he was using the most sickening and disparaging terms to describe them. I really was shocked. I took him aside and explained to him that there was only one thing separating him from them and that was a serious hit to the head, a real possibility with the life he was living. Well really it was two, the grace and mercy of God was the second, but I don't think that they rated very highly in his consideration of life. Instead, for anyone who lives for Christ, compassion, sympathy and understanding for the weak should motivate our actions.

For a minister, the grace and mercy that they received should be front and center in any consideration of their dealing with the weak. Of course, weakness comes in many forms. I have spoken above more about intellectual weakness, but we could have been talking equally about physical, emotional, or spiritual weakness. For members it is no different.

The Servant of All

²⁰ Then the mother of the sons of Zebedee came to Jesus with her sons, bowing down and making a request of Him. ²¹ And He said to her, "What do you desire?" She said to Him, "Say that in Your kingdom these two sons of mine shall sit, one at Your right, and one at Your left." ²² But Jesus replied, "You do not know what you are asking. Are you able to drink the cup that I am about to drink?" They said to Him, "We are able." ²³ He said to them, "My cup you shall drink; but to sit at My right and at My left is not Mine to give, but it is for those for whom it has been prepared by My Father."

²⁴ And after hearing this, the other ten disciples became indignant with the two brothers. ²⁵ But Jesus called them to Himself and said, "You know that the rulers of the Gentiles domineer over them, and those in high position exercise authority over them. ²⁶ It is not this way among you, but whoever wants to become prominent among you shall be your servant, ²⁷ and whoever desires to be first among you shall be your slave; ²⁸ just as the Son of Man did not come to be served, but to serve, and to give His life as a ransom for many."

—MATT 20:20–28

MY GRANDFATHER ALSO BUILT our local Anglican church, a small but attractive timber structure and this time fortunately without incident. In the 1960's, one of the local girls married an Anglican priest who then went on to be the bishop in Port Moresby in Papua New Guinea. Soon after, the local Anglicans decided it was time to upgrade from timber to brick and build a new church. The architect, buoyed by this bit of local knowledge, decided to draw his inspiration for the building from a New Guinea spirit house where who knows what ungodly practices are carried on. However, as a building, it functions well and is architecturally pleasing. To honor such an auspicious occasion and connection, the bishop sent over a memento for the locals, a stone. Now that stone had been used by a local witchdoctor in his occult practices and it was set up on a plaque in pride of place in the building. Over the course of time, a later priest and a licensed lay preacher took that stone, burnt it, and smashed it to dust and good on them. What has light to do with darkness?

The archbishop in Brisbane was horrified, "You have offended my mate the bishop," and promptly took the license to preach from the layman and tore strips off the priest with all manner of threats. In a minister's fraternal meeting my friend and mentor, the Lutheran pastor at the time, berated the poor priest for bowing to a bishop in face of a clear gospel issue. He replied, "Don't you obey your bishop?" And his answer was, "No! Our Bishop does what we ask him to do." I have since got to know that Lutheran bishop well and now realize that a truer word has never been spoken. As for the archbishop, he went on to the nation's highest office, Governor General, but resigned in disgrace when it was revealed that he had allowed a known pedophile priest to remain in office. He would be forced to apologize to victims for not pursuing their claims more rigorously.[1]

The story I have just recounted is the tale of a man in high office who had lost his vision of what it was to be a servant to all. The content of this chapter is Jesus' clear teaching of the pastor being a servant which can be a hard lesson to learn and even harder to continue to maintain over a lifetime. However, it is never beneath our dignity or our faith and our office to be a servant. It is

1. Horn and Field, "Child Abuse," par 1–20.

the foundation on which Christian leadership is built and not just leadership but Christianity itself. No one is worthy of higher office if their ministry is not built and continues to be built on the attitude of servanthood and its associated humility. This was the example set by Jesus, our example who was prophesied in Isaiah to be the suffering servant, not the triumphant king. That day will come. In the meantime, Jesus clearly taught that he expected no less of his disciples. In the twenty-second chapter of Luke's gospel, after Jesus washed his disciples' feet we read:

> 24 And a dispute also developed among them as to which one of them was regarded as being the greatest. 25 And He said to them, "The kings of the Gentiles domineer over them; and those who have authority over them are called 'Benefactors.' 26 But it is not this way for you; rather, the one who is the greatest among you must become like the youngest, and the leader like the servant. 27 For who is greater, the one who reclines at the table or the one who serves? Is it not the one who reclines at the table? But I am among you as the one who serves.

A servant yet far from a servant. While Jesus did gird a towel around his waist and wash his disciples' feet, on that very night, like many other days and nights he did also recline at the table as the guest of honor. It is the dichotomy of being at the same time both a servant and a leader worthy of double honor that can be so difficult. Yet, Paul said of Jesus' attitude and what should also be ours, "5 Have this attitude in yourselves, which was also in Christ Jesus, 6 who, as He *already* existed in the form of God, did not consider equality with God something to be grasped, 7 but emptied Himself *by* taking the form of a bond-servant *and* being born in the likeness of men. 8 And being found in appearance as a man, He humbled Himself by becoming obedient to the point of death: death on a cross" (Phil 2:5–8).

So, how does this dual and apparently contradictory role demonstrate itself in the same person? Let's go back a step and consider the role of people with "less important" duties in a church. The rise to higher office in the church would frequently be started on the first rung of the ladder, as a "deacon." It is not a complicated word;

it is simply a Greek word that means "servant." The first reference to deacons is found in Acts 6:1–6:

> Now at this time, as the disciples were increasing in number, a complaint developed on the part of the Hellenistic Jews against the native Hebrews, because their widows were being overlooked in the daily serving of food. 2 So the twelve summoned the congregation of the disciples and said, "It is not desirable for us to neglect the word of God in order to serve tables. 3 Instead, brothers and sisters, select from among you seven men of good reputation, full of the Spirit and of wisdom, whom we may put in charge of this task. 4 But we will devote ourselves to prayer and to the ministry of the word." 5 The announcement found approval with the whole congregation; and they chose Stephen, a man full of faith and of the Holy Spirit, and Philip, Prochorus, Nicanor, Timon, Parmenas, and Nicolas, a proselyte from Antioch. 6 And they brought these men before the apostles; and after praying, they laid their hands on them.

These were not deacons like any I know. They are full of the Holy Spirit and Stephen could preach with such power that the hardest of hearts were moved, (in the wrong way unfortunately). Stephen could perform wonders and signs (Acts 7:8) and also had a radical theology of faith. His sermon to the Sanhedrin is the longest in the Book of Acts and its content was possibly more radical than that of the apostles at that stage. Paul was Stephen's reluctant disciple. Yet despite all that, they were set aside to be servants of the neediest and least liked in the Jerusalem church, the foreign widows. This job was unwanted by the apostles as they had the much too important spiritual work of prayer and ministry of the word to do, and it was important. The apostles on their part did not have a rigid job description for the deacons and allowed room for the deacons' gifts to operate and develop.

Paul wasn't always in complete agreement with the church in Jerusalem and perhaps the ministry of the word was not quite as important as the Apostles maintained. Twice he neglected the ministry of the word to "wait on tables" as he ensured that charitable donations safely reached the Jerusalem church. As for Paul's qualification for deacons in the church in Ephesus, as opposed to the Apostles in Jerusalem, there is no mention that they needed to be "filled with the Spirit." In Jerusalem, who these men were was obvious, but just a few years later it had become muddied. The problem with saying, "I am full of the Spirit," is that it is so subjective. Across the Aegean Sea in Corinth, it would appear that the church had its full quota and then some more of men and presumably women who were "full of the Spirit" and his power. All the gifts were evident there, prophecy, speaking in tongues, and the interpretation of tongues, words of knowledge. Yes, the Corinthians had them all and more. And I am not decrying that, but they also had conflict, immorality, and thoughtless disregard for one another. In short, they were lacking the humility of a servant.

How could such a church, and any church, really know if something was a manifestation of the Spirit and not merely self-indulgence? As Luther said of such people, they "had swallowed the Holy Spirit, feathers and all." The qualifications that Paul gave for this first rung on the ladder are not so much about being "full of the Spirit" but about being led by him and allowing him to model their character till they were such people that they reflected Christ. Perhaps ultimately, that is the best test of whether one is "full of the Spirit." And that is definitely not a male only prerogative.

There was initially an expectancy that Jesus would return in the lifetime of the Apostles, but it was becoming increasingly obvious to Paul that that was not going to happen. The letters to Timothy and Titus were about setting up the church for the long haul. Those apostles that had seen Jesus were dying. Paul could say, "be imitators of me as I am of Christ." But he will soon die so who then do they imitate? The one task, if not the most important task for an elder in this church is to live a life that is so exemplary that it shows us what Christ is like. Every church, even the smallest, needs such people and they are recognized as such with the title "Elder." These small churches may not need much in the work of administration, but Paul's guidelines are not qualifications to be rulers but to be role models.

Yet I was not talking about elders, but about deacons who are one rung down the ladder. The one thing that a church cannot do is to say, "They are only the deacons. It does not matter much if we get it wrong." Deacons were to be appointed with the same care as elders as they are the future of the church and is a reminder that ministry is concerned with generation, not months or years. The qualifications for deacons are only slightly less, if even at all less than those of an elder and like the role of an elder, their role was not defined. But I will attempt to define what it is for a deacon. It is simply an apprentice elder. It is a time of being under closer scrutiny where their ministry can develop. This is why a church's choice of deacon is important. An elder or a pastor or a bishop or even an archbishop should never graduate from being a deacon. Paul was very pleased to call himself a deacon (Rom 1:1) and even a slave and used both words of Timothy (1 Tim 4:6). You should not get promoted to be an elder or a pastor or a bishop or to be anything else without still remaining a servant or a deacon at its core. This is the very clear teaching of Jesus and the whole of the New Testament.

The idea of servant leadership is also exceptionally good advice for the secular world as well. Before the coming of the gospel, heroes dominated the world. We can think of generals like Alexander and Julius Caesar who acquired great prestige and honor through bloodshed, brutal victories, and intrigues. We can also think of the brutal dictatorial reign of emperors who amassed riches and required subservience from those they ruled. The Christian virtue of servanthood should be the natural possession of military and politics when a community has been Christianized. General Bruce Clarke[2] put this Christian understanding in military terms, "Rank is given you to enable you to better serve those above and below you. It is not given for you to practice your idiosyncrasies." It is hard to imagine the horrors of the Somme originating from leadership with such values. As for politics, the term "Prime Minister" means first servant and some politicians do embody a life of often thankless service.

Paul expressed this life of a servant by working as a tentmaker so no one had to support him which allowed him to proclaim the gospel free to all who would listen. Barnabas, his partner in

2. This career soldier rose to command the United States Army in Europe from 1960 to 1962,

evangelism also had the same practice. Yet, this was not a community of faith without money. Tyrannus would have wanted payment for the hire of his lecture hall, widows were supported, and offerings were sent to the Jerusalem church, However, as for Paul, he worked at secular employment and supported himself. (Read First Corinthians chapter 9 where he explains his practice and the reason behind it). How few of us would have a mind and the stamina that we could work hard and still find the time to preach and be an evangelist and pastor. The life of servanthood will find different expressions dependent on the natural abilities, gifts, and the financial position of the person. We are not all the same and Paul was not critical of the apostles for travelling with their wives and being supported in their ministry. Neither was servanthood such that he would stop others having the joy of serving him as when he received an offering from the Philippian church.

Does this mean that the pastor is at the beck and call of all and sundry? Yes, it can. The humility that comes with seeing yourself as no better than anyone else whatever your status, and the compassion that that should come from having Christ's life in you should make you readily available. This aught not be because it is your Christian duty but because it should be your nature. As Jesus healed ten lepers and only the Samaritan returned to thank him, so a life of service will often be thankless, but we were not called to a life of accolades but of humbly and self-sacrificingly showing what Jesus is like. Yet, how little we model Christ. As I said earlier, when Jesus walked on this earth our heavenly father allowed ungodly men to respond to his son's service by permitting them to vent their fury without limit. His only crime was simply that his holiness and his works exposed their sinfulness. Very few of us will be called to walk such a path as a consequence of our service.

This could all sound like a burden, but is it? For many years we would close our Gideon meetings by standing in a circle while holding hands and singing, *Blest be the Tie that Binds*. The story behind that illustrates how serving should not be a burden. John Fawcett and his family moved to Wainsgate in Yorkshire in 1765 to be the pastor at Baptist chapel there. His community was described this way, "The people were all farmers and shepherds, poor as Job's turkey; an uncouth lot whose speech one could hardly understand, unable to read or write; most of them pagans, cursed with vice and ignorance and wild tempers. The Established Church had never touched them; only the humble Baptists had sent an itinerant preacher there and he had made a good beginning."[3] The Fawcetts' flock were so poor that frequently he was paid in kind. It was a time of extreme privation, yet he had made a name for himself as a preacher and theologian.

After seven years he received and accepted a call from a London church which would have changed his life. His "farewell sermon had been preached, the wagon was loaded when love and tears prevailed and [he] sacrificed the attraction of a London pulpit to the affections of his poor, but devoted flock."[4] The next Sunday his text was Luke 12:15, "Beware, and be on your guard against every form of greed; for not *even* when one is affluent does his life consist of his possessions." At the conclusion of the service the congregation sang the hymn he had written the previous night. Fawcett would serve that impoverished community for fifty-four years yet still received national and international recognition. However, that is another story.

Another illustration of this point is from James Stalker, a minister in Scotland from the end of the nineteenth century. He wrote. "When I first was settled in a church, I discovered a thing of which nobody had told me, and which I had not anticipated, but proved to be a tremendous aid in doing the work of ministry. I fell in love with my congregation. I do not know how otherwise to express it. It was as genuine a blossom of the heart as any which I have ever experienced. It made it easy to do anything for my people."[5]

A minister who does not love his flock and serves them has no place behind their pulpit. A member who does not love those he worships with, nor readily serves them, should question if they are doing more harm than good by staying.

3. Bailey, *The Gospel*, 136.

4. Julian, *Dictionary*, 148.

5. Stalker, *The Preacher*, 231.

Someone Who Listens

> My dear brothers and sisters, take note of this: Everyone should
> be quick to listen, slow to speak and slow to become angry.

> —Jas 1:19

In Australia there is a common greeting, "How y' going?" and the reply is invariably, "No point complaining." A response to that might then be, "No. Nobody listens." The banter might continue something like, "Another married man?" but I invariably respond, "The only person who listens charges by the hour." While all this is just lighthearted conversation among friends perhaps it may also be a case that many a true word is said in jest. Learning to listen is the most important thing a minister can do. It is the most important thing any Christian can do. If he/she cannot listen to the person in front of them, whose burdens they are called to share, it begs the question of whether they will be able to hear when their master speaks.

Years of theological training should give a person a reason to hold to their Christian belief and equip then to deliver a theological answer when needed, but how often is that what is needed? This point was made by one of the sounding boards I used when writing this book. The man was a very senior pastor and denominational administrator. He told me how a woman once asked him what God thought of murderers. It would have been easy to answer that theologically, but he had the perception to ask, "Why is that question important to you?" It transpired that the woman had had an abortion and was living with the guilt of it. Without taking time to listen, the discussion could have been one that further compounded the awareness the woman already had of her sin. Instead, it turned to one of forgiveness and life. He lamented how theological colleges did not train students how to listen.

When I was doing my necessary Google search on what the Bible says about listening to someone, I found the following quote of Dietrich Bonhoeffer on a number of sites:

> There is a kind of listening with half an ear that presumes already to know what the other person has to say. It is an impatient, inattentive listening, that despises the brother and is only waiting for a chance to speak and thus get rid of the other person. This is no fulfillment of our obligation, and it is certain that here too our attitude toward our brother only reflects our relationship to God.[1]

I am afraid I had forgotten it. It comes from his book *Life Together*, which I read back in 1974 when I was in Bible college, so I suppose there is an excuse. Back then, that book played a large part in forming the way I thought about the church and church life. Most sites just quote this passage and move on, but I will stay and explore it further. Much later, I learnt the circumstances that *Life Together* was written under, so I knew that there was at least one seminary where its pupils were taught to listen. From 1937 to 1939[2] during the prequel to and into the Second World War, Bonhoeffer ran a clandestine seminary for the Confessing Church in Germany. That group was a kickback against Nazi control of the Christian church in Germany.

Can you imagine what their trainee pastors were asked to listen to? In the darkness of that bitter war, it would have been about hate, privations, battlefield death and injury, missing loved ones. Where is a theological answer, no matter how correct, to placate and calm a questioner let alone be a balm in the extremes that were to follow as the war turned against Germany? Is such an answer even wanted most times? Imagine a pastor inwardly trying to

---

1. Bonhoeffer, *Life Together*, 75–6.
2. Metaxas, *Bonhoeffer*, 298–300, 360.

absorb and give comfort when he would have his own unanswered questions of equal horror. And yet, that is exactly what he taught his seminarians. Yes, there is a place for the theological answer but getting the timing right is crucial, especially then, when the listener may have been an informer. However, listening does not need any special timing, but it does need skill.

We should listen because listening is an act of love. Bonhoeffer saw how our love for our Heavenly Father began to grow by listening to his word, and reasoned that in the same way, so our love for our brother or sister should grow by listening to them. He saw how pastors often think they must contribute when instead their greatest service may be just listening. He understood how a person who no longer listens to his brother will soon lose the ability to hear from God and "be doing nothing but prattle in the presence of God too. . . . and in the end, there is nothing left but spiritual chatter and clerical condescension arrayed in pious words."[3]

Bonhoeffer was right when he saw the first service that a pastor owes to the fellowship that he/she leads is to listen long and hard to them. A pastor who thinks that his/her time is too valuable to keep quiet and listen will eventually find that time too valuable to even share with God.[4] But this is not a warning only for pastors as it a warning for all Christians. For all of us, our ability to listen to each other reflects our ability to listen to our Lord. Only when we listen with God's ears can we hope to speak with God's lips.

So, how do we learn to listen? Obviously, put yourself in a position where you have the opportunity to listen. My personal situation means that visiting is not as easy as I would like but we have an open door at our home. People know that if the car is in the carport, we are home, and a cup of tea is only a few minutes away (and that is not a dreadful teabag but a properly brewed strong pot) along with a listening ear. Sometimes I am busy, but no task is so important that I cannot get away for enough time to share a "cuppa" and a biscuit. Even the most intense work benefits from the break. Sometimes, I do have to ask the Lord to help me make up the time,

---

3. Bonhoeffer, *Life Together*, 75.
4. Bonhoeffer, *Life Together*, 75.

which he does, because my visitor is important to him as well as us. In these situations, after excusing myself, my dear wife takes over the role of listener.

But what about the minister? My friend who I mentioned earlier in this chapter spoke of his observation when reviewing the annual statistics each church returned. Like every denomination, sadly, there were some churches that declined and others that had plateaued but, again like the other groups, there were those that were growing. Without fail, those were the ones where there was a strong focus on visitation. When I studied to be a pastor, it was drummed into us, visit, visit, visit! You won't get to know your congregation standing behind the pulpit, but you will do it at the kitchen table over a cup of tea. We were taught, organize your day so your morning is kept for prayer, Bible study and sermon preparation and guard it jealously. Your afternoons are to be set aside for visiting. Now it is becoming very popular to meet for coffee and I have definitely become a coffee snob in my advancing years, and there is a place for that, but it should not be the primary way of visiting. A public setting will not allow for the most intimate of conversations. This can only be done back at the kitchen table. It is not likely to happen on the first visit either.

What should prompt a visit from the pastor? Life is what happens when people are making other plans, so they say, and the joys of a new birth, or a marriage are to be shared. Likewise, the sorrow of a death or serious accident or bad health diagnosis. But these should be the extraordinary visits, not what seem now to be the ordinary. Regular visitation is critical but how we visit is just as important as how we listen. Another friend has often commented about one pastor of whom he said, "He always had an agenda when he visited, he usually wanted to borrow something." From the number of times that I have heard him repeat this, it has obviously had a lasting impact. Know your congregation, talk to them about suitable times. In my farming community an evening visit is simply out of the question and don't come near them at all during potato harvest. Others might be night owls and don't care how late you arrive. But to know so little about your congregation that you plan a visit to a farmer at eight in the evening when he will be up before dawn is seriously deficient.

For most of your flock, to visit, just to listen, and then perhaps to speak will be the greatest service you can give. Surely, after what is said about preaching to the heart that would be the most important service? But if you don't know their heart, how can you preach to it and apply the comfort of God's word?

What Really Goes Wrong

For many are called, but few are chosen.

—MATT 22:14

WHAT DID JESUS MEAN when he said that many are called but few are chosen? It puzzled me for years and still does and I would not be Robinson Crusoe in this. However, consider this . . . how many have been called to a life of humility and service but think they are especially favored by God and have been chosen for some special work beyond that of the call of others. One of the most difficult times of my life was when I was part of the disastrous choice of pastor. I was not in the service when the prospective pastor came to preach with a view to a call. Everyone told me how wonderful he was, but I had a great disquiet about him. Eventually, I was persuaded against my will to ignore that inner voice and to be honest I could not pinpoint what was causing me to be unsure. In three months, the church had almost halved in attendance. He was a dreadful pastor but, in his mind, that did not matter as he now claimed to be a prophet. So, he did not have to be a good pastor as that was not what he had been called to be. On top of that, he had reached sinless perfection and was on a spiritual plane above lesser sinning mortals. None of this came out in his interview with the elders! I am afraid my halo slipped one day, but it gave me a great deal of satisfaction to say, "You think you are a living prophet, but I think you are a dead loss." As an elder, I felt responsible for this mess and tried to do what I could to stand between this man and the damage he was doing to the church. It almost crushed me. After this pastor appointed a new board, he simply cancelled my membership and, by so doing, removed a tremendous burden from me. God forbid that you will ever encounter such a man.

I expect that the issues you will encounter will not be as extreme as those which I considered myself responsible for. What really goes wrong? This is not something that can be broken down into an us and them mentality drawn over denominational boundaries. My observation in this final chapter applies across all groups. It would take a lifetime to explore this subject, and our time would be better spent considering what has gone right. But the simple fact remains that some pastors and some churches harm rather than grow their members in grace and Christlikeness. You don't have to look too far to see stories that simply defy belief. In Australia, and many places in the west, scandals that were the hidden dirty secrets of denominations and its leadership have been exposed for all to see. This has brought reproach upon all Christians, of whom the vast majority just want to get on and live a life honoring to God.

While the aberrations vary in degree, it has been going on from the earliest days of the church. We read about it first occurring in Jerusalem when there was discrimination against the widows of Greek speaking Jews. Paul, not too many years later would say of the Corinthian church that their services do more harm than good (1 Cor 11:17). You don't have to read much church history to be sickened to your stomach at the violence, intolerance and hatred that so quickly replaced peace, tolerance, and love. How quickly the church and its ministers have rejected the fruit of the Spirit for the deeds of the prince of this world!

So, what really goes wrong and what makes a man or woman inappropriate and unsuitable for the role of shepherd? Some of this has already been touched upon. Fortunately, there are people who still long to hear God's word spoken and explained and communicated to them. Yet not everyone is an eloquent public speaker, and some ministers simply have difficulty communicating. That person can be the nicest person you could meet on a one-to-one basis, but it means little if he/she just stands behind the pulpit and mumbles to his/her congregation. It also means little if he/she has a loud clear voice that is easy to hear and understand but if his/her thoughts are so disorganized that people walk away perplexed and wondering what was trying to be said. As I maintain in the chapter on preaching to the heart, the mechanics of preaching can be learned, and it behooves a minister of the gospel to master his craft. One of the tools recommended to me is Toastmasters. There is no point in working hard to gain knowledge and praying long to receive insights if the words drop to the floor between the pulpit and the first row of seats. I have suggested that a collective amnesia has come over the church where it has forgotten what preaching has been, can be and is meant to be.

I have also spoken about not placing a pastor to a pinnacle above that which the Lord intended. Whatever life may have been like in New Testament times or in other cultures, we in the west live in an individualistic and democratic community. The days have long gone where a pastor had respect automatically given to him. Once he, and it was only a "he" back then, would have been one of the few people in the community with an advanced education and this set him apart. Trust and respect now must be earned, and it always should have been. This is done on a person-to-person basis which takes time and conscious action. Visitation is vitally important for church growth. If you will not commit to it, I suggest you seek a different vocation. Remember, there is a world of difference between asking why someone has not attended church to letting them know they have been missed. Visit to listen and not to speak and be slow to offer theological answers as most will know them already. In a sense, a pastor should be more like a psychologist who listens, but unlike a psychologist he/she should be Spirit led to ask probing questions, so the member understands the issue themselves.

Respected, yes hopefully you have earned this, Loved, again hopefully you have earned the right to be loved, but the burden is also upon the minister to see their member's vocation as important, respected and God honoring also, and to love them. When ministers allow their role to be seen as befitting only the most spiritual and favored by God, people will not have the courage to talk to their pastor directly about perceived shortcomings in their ministry. A friend had issues with a priest in town. To put him in his place, that priest drew him a picture of a wheel with a rim, spokes, and a hub and the explained it for the benefit of my poor ignorant friend. The hub was God, and the rim was my friend and never the twain shall meet except for the priest who was the spokes that connects man with God. How could anyone talk to such a man?

My old mentor asked me a question, "What separates me as a minister from my members?" He answered it from a Lutheran perspective, and that was, "Very little." Yes, he had been set aside to minister the word and sacrament but that was all. His members can pray, visit the sick, do good deeds, evangelize and any of the myriad of other things that make up Christian life and ministry. They can even go boldly before God's throne without any assistance from him. Not only did he believe it, but he encouraged and reinforced this in his congregation. Humility must be evident in the minister along with an elevated view of the ministry of the members for there to be good communication between pastor and congregation. It must be a two-way street.

One of my employees went off to train to be a minister. After finishing his theological degree, he had to complete a secular degree before he could be ordained in that denomination. To put food on the table, he came back to work for me for two days a week. Unfortunately, he injured himself at work and I went with him to John, our company doctor, who was also an elder in my church. After a few stitches, the doctor said to him, "Ted has a workplace rehabilitation program in place so I will have to assess you for light duties." My employee said, "That won't be necessary John as I am only working two days a week." I chipped in, "That's right John, he is studying for the ministry and preparing himself for only working one day a week!" The poor old nurse rolled her eyes, but John could see the humor while knowing too well that this can be the perception and sometimes the reality.

A pastor works largely unsupervised with little close scrutiny of how he/she spends his/her time. I know when I did my training, there was little attention to the mechanics of pastoral ministry. It is necessary to have a clear plan for the week. As a general principle, I was told to keep your morning for prayer and Bible study and the afternoon for visitation. In the busyness of life, it is easy to let one or even all of these slide. Failing to be intentional means that things that are important to the life of the church may not get done.

My own church is situated in the middle of a potato field with farmers or retired farmers as its backbone. Others are businessmen or retired businessmen. The one thing we have in common is that we work, or have worked, long hours, six days a week. We are accustomed to hard work, physically and/or mentally. Apart from the preaching, our services are run by the laypeople with the pastor only taking a turn in the different roles in the service. The preparation for this lay involvement is after a tiring day when they should have been resting.

I don't know what it is like in a city church, but country folk cannot understand how the ministry can be seen as a nine to five job with a full day or even two off where you do not attend to church matters. It is not a luxury they get. The ministry is no place for snowflakes that melt at the sight of hard work. It should never be forgotten that humans have a capacity for hard work, and on top of this, the Lord has promised his strength for the task. When you read early Australian church history there can be little doubt that the hardest working of us have life fairly easy. Where is the resilience we read of in our pioneering pastors? Another wise man once said, "When the Lord finds a willing horse, the Devil will flog him to death." There is a lot of truth in it but someone who lives a Spirit led life draws on strength that is beyond him/her. That same Spirit, when listened to, will say when to rest.

When pastors commence ministry in a location, they can't avoid having something in their mind about what a church should be like. All this can be good in and of itself, yet it can still be wrong. Each church has its own character. My Baptist church at Tenthill is only ten minutes' drive from the Baptist Church in Gatton, my hometown. A business management consultant would say there is no justification for two churches when the population is so mobile. It might be different if we still travelled on horseback. Look at the cost saving by amalgamating. Yet the two churches are as different as chalk and cheese. For someone to come along and put all of that distinctiveness in the bin and start again would be to deny what

God had been doing in each church for generations. It is important to discover what a church appreciates and what they consider important, and you won't learn this in under six months. What is distinctive and good needs to be built upon and developed, not minimized.

My church appreciates food! A first-time attender to Gatton Baptist will be given a tea bag tea in a disposable cup and a dry biscuit (sorry friends, but it is true) but come to Tenthill and you will be given a full color cookbook written by the members and a piece of homemade sponge cake and a savory scone for starters. Your tea will be served from a teapot into a china cup. Feedback from visitors seeking a church has been that, while other churches do try to make you feel welcome, it can feel forced. The naturalness of conversation over a magnificent spread makes welcoming so natural. But we are more than sponge cake as there is a long history of ministry to the young, with members giving sacrificially to employ a youth pastor and of generous missions' support. The pastor must take time to understand his congregation seeking to build upon the foundation already laid rather than tearing it down to rebuild in its place whatever he/she thinks is important.

Again, I have only touched on the subject. Very likely, each church that has been through a difficult time would contribute additional topics. Anyone who lives a life free of church drama at some time is blessed. Should you encounter troubles, it is very easy to throw up your hands in horror and walk away and, to be truthful, many have. I could have easily done this and would have were it not for the grace of our loving savior. The memory of those who served well and the knowledge of what can go right sustained me. Christ loved his church and gave his life for it. He loved it with all its failings and imperfections. He asks no more of us than we serve and love and forgive. And heaven knows, there is a lot to forgive.

Questions to Ask a Potential Pastor

NO DOUBT YOU WILL have questions of your own about doctrinal beliefs and denomination distinctives, and I do not want to diminish the importance of that, but these might not be the most important questions. The one thing that the Book of Job shows is that the Lord was happier with some honest heresy from Job than he was with the rigid compassionless orthodoxy of his miserable comforters. You need to delve deeply into who this man or woman really is, not only what he says he believes. You must determine if the person applying for the role is someone who will fall in love with his church, who will serve and not rule them, and graciously bring them along with him/her to the source of all grace.

Based on the earlier chapters I have written some questions that you might like to consider rewording for your own particular needs.

Questions based on *A Vocation not a Profession:*

1. How do you understand the difference between the role of pastor as a profession and a vocation?
2. How do you see the spirituality of your calling to say that of a farmer or accountant or businessman?

Questions based on *Integrity and Gifting:*

1. Who mentored you, and what was he/she like?
2. Tell us about your prayer life and of an answer to prayer.

3. Tell us about a situation that caused you to question the love of God, and how you dealt with it?

Questions based on *The Importance of Developing a Strong Character:*

1. How do you see the difference between having integrity and strength of character?
2. What area of Christian/social justice evokes a strong response in you?

Questions based on *Preaching to the Heart and not the Head:*

1. How important do you see the role of preaching?
2. What efforts have you taken to master your craft beyond seminary lessons?
3. Give an example of when the Lord blessed your preaching.

Question based on *A person of Undivided Attention:*

1. What steps are you taking to own a home on retirement?

Questions based on *A Person with Compassion for the Weak:*

1. What experience have you had with people who are different e.g., intellectual difficulties?
2. How has that affected your behavior?

Question based on *The Servant of All:*

1. How do you understand the role of pastor as servant?

Questions based on *Someone who Listens:*

1. How important do you see the role of visitation?
2. Below what level of visitation should the elders become concerned and talk to you?

Questions based on *What Really Goes Wrong:*

1. You will be working unsupervised. How will you plan your day?
2. The contribution to church life by some of your members will be made after a long day's work. What is your attitude to intrusions into your day off for church matters?
3. How many hours a day do you consider reasonable to work on church matters?
4. Do you plan to make immediate changes before you get to know what is of concern to your members?

Bibliography

Allen, Matthew. "Samuel Marsden—A Contested Life." In *The History of Tasmania Vol. 2*, by John West, 166–67. Launceston: H. Dowling, 1852.

Augustine. *Augustine: Confessions and Enchiridion*. Translated by Albert C. Outler. Philadelphia: Westminster, 1955.

Averill, Lloyd. *Go North Young Man*. Springwood: Lloyd Averill, 1992.

Bailey, Albert. *The Gospel in Hymns*. New York: Scribner, 1950.

Barclay, William. *The Plain Man Looks at the Lord's Prayer*. London: Fontana, 1964.

Bonhoeffer, Dietrich. *Life Together*. Translated by John W. Doberstein. London: SCM, 1972.

Boultbee, T. P. *An Introduction to the Theology of the Church of England*. London: Longman Green, 1895.

Catholic Online. *St. Thomas Aquinas*. n.d. https://www.catholic.org/saints/saint.php?saint_id=253.

Chant, Barry. *Heart of Fire*. Unley Park: Tabor, 1984.

———. "The Spirit of Pentecost: Origins and Development of the Pentecostal Movement in Australia 1870–1939." PhD diss., Macquarie University., n.d.

Christianity Today. "Charles Finney: Father of American Revivalism." https://www.christianitytoday.com/history/people/evangelistsandapologists/charles-finney.html.

Cross, Whitney R. *The Burned Over District: The Social and Intellectual History of Enthusastic Religion in Western New York, 1800–1850*. Ithaca: Cornrll University Press, 1982.

Fee, G. D. *Corinthians: A Study Guide*. Brussels: International Correspondence Institute, 1979.

Edwards, Jonathan. "Sinners in the Hands of an Angry God." In *A Casebook*, edited by Wilson H. Kimnach et al., ##–##. New Haven: Yale University Press, 2010.

"Evangelistic and Healing Campaign: Amazing Scenes." *Cessnock Eagle*, June 25, 1929.

Friedenthal, Richard. *Luther*. London: Weidenfeld and Nicolson, 1967.

Gladwin, Michael. "Flogging Parsons? Australian Anglican Clergymen the Magistracy, and Convicts, 1788–1850." *Journal of Religious History* 36 (2012) 386–403.

Graham, Billy. *Just as I Am.* Sydney: Harper Collins, 1997.

Horn, Allyson, and Donna Field. "Child Abuse Royal Commission: Peter Hollingworth, Former Governor-General and Anglican Archbishop Apologises to Victims of Paedophile Teachers." *ABC News,* Nov 13, 2015. https://www.abc.net.au/news/2015-11-13/peter-hollingworth-says-sorry-to-victims-child-abuse-brisbane/6939804.

Hunt, Stan. *The Assemblies of God, Queensland Conference.* Brisbane: Assembly, U.D.

Julian, John. *A Dictionary of Hymnology, Vol. 1.* New York: Dover, 1907.

Lancaster, Janet. "First Impressions." *Good News,* May 1926.

———. "The Good News." *Good News,* September 1926.

———. "The Good News." *Good News,* November 1926.

———. "Good News." *Good News,* May 1927.

Manning, Roger B. "The Spread of the Popular Reformation in England." *The Sixteenth Century Journal* 1 (1970) 35–52.

Marsden, George A. *Jonathan Edwards: A Life.* New Haven: Yale University Press, 2003.

Marsden, Samuel. "SMarsden Sermons 01 to 98>Revelations 3_2 (Sermon 24)." *Moore Theological College.* n.d. https://moorecollege.access.preservica.com/IO_580d2007-8668-44b3-8199-1cd346801b98/.

McKlung, Grant. *Azusa Street and Beyond.* South Plainfield: Logos, 1986.

Meier, Christian. *Julius Caesar.* London: Folio, 2004.

Metaxas, Eric. *Bonhoeffer.* Nashville: Thomas Nelson, 2010.

———. *Martin Luther.* New York: Viking, 2017.

Morgan, J. J. *The '59 Revival in Wales, Some Incidents in the Life and Work of David Morgan Ysbytty.* Mould: Morgan, 1909.

Nichol, John T. *The Pentecostals.* Plainfield: Logos, 1971.

Piggin, Stuart. *Firestorm of the Lord.* Carlisle: Paternoster, 2000.

———. *The Fount of Public Prosperity.* Clayton: Monash University Publishing, 2018.

———. *Spirit, Word and World: Evangelical Christianity in Australia.* Brunswic East: Acorn, 2012.

Schwartz, Hans. "Martin Luther's Understanding of Vocation in the Light of Today's Problems." *Lutheran Theological Journal* 30 (1996) 4–12.

Spurgeon, Charles. *Lectures to My Students.* New York: Carter, 1890.

Stalker, James. *The Preacher and His Models.* London: Hodder & Stoughton, 1891.

Stott, John. *Calling Christian Leaders.* London: InterVarsity, 2002.

Taylor, William G. *Pathfinders of the Great South Land.* London: Epworth, n.d.

Thielicke, Helmut. *The Ethics of Sex.* Translated by John W. Doberstein. New York: Harper & Row, 1964.

Tracey, Joseph. *The Great Awakening: A History of Revivals of Religion in the Times of Edwards and Whitfield*. Edinburgh: Banner of Truth, 1976.

Van Eyk, Frederick. "The South African Evangelist's Report, May 15, 1928." *Good News*, June 1926.

Wesley, John. *The Journal of John Wesley*. Chicago: Moody, 1974.

Westminster Abby. *William Wilberforce and Family*. n.d. https://www.westminster-abbey.org/abbey-commemorations/commemorations/william-wilberforce-family#:~:text=William%20Wilberforce%20was%20buried%20in%20the%20north%20transept,The%20family%20had%20long%20been%20settled%20in%20Yorkshire.